THE
GROWTH
MINDSET

CLASSROOM-READY
RESOURCE BOOK

A Teacher's Toolkit for Encouraging Grit and Resilience in All Students

Annie Brock and Heather Hundley

Published by:
Ulysses Press
P. O. Box 3440
Berkeley, CA 94703
www.ulyssespress.com

ISBN13: 978-1-64604-044-5
Library of Congress Control Number: 2020931866

Printed in Canada
10 9 8 7 6 5 4

Acquisitions editor: Casie Vogel
Managing editor: Claire Chun
Editor: Renee Rutledge
Proofreader: Barbara Schultz
Cover design: what!design @ whatweb.com
Interior design: Jake Flaherty
Interior art: page 92 "My Wife and My Mother-in-Law" by William Ely Hill/Wikimedia Commons; "Duck-Rabbit" (no attribution)/Wikimedia Commons; Faces by Edgar Rubin

CONTENTS

INTRODUCTION

In *The Growth Mindset Coach*, we produced a chapter-a-month guidebook for cultivating growth mind-sets in your classroom. In *The Growth Mindset Playbook,* we dug deeper into how classrooms and schools can empower students and increase achievement through building growth mindsets. In this new addi-tion to our Growth Mindset series, we are expanding these ideas by offering turnkey lessons (ranging from 15 minutes to an hour) to use in your classroom. We'll revisit the same subject matter from our previous books and offer 45 valuable, ready-to-teach lessons and over 50 reproducible resources that will help you put the power of growth mindset to work for you and your students.

Each of our lessons will have a simple structure:

TEACHER TALK
A pre-lesson summary of the purpose of the lesson.

LEARNING OBJECTIVE
What the students should know or do by the end of the lesson.

RESOURCES AND MATERIALS
The resources and materials necessary to conduct the lesson.

METHOD
Step-by-step instructions for lesson implementation.

CHECK FOR UNDERSTANDING
Ideas to check for understanding during and after the lesson.

SUPPLEMENTAL/EXTENSION IDEAS
We have also included a section after each lesson that offers simple ideas to supplement the objective. These supplements might include ideas for student displays, read-aloud books, or other materials that

will supplement the lesson in some meaningful way. You can choose to use these or not; the supplements are not essential to the lesson itself.

Additionally, in the methodology of the lesson plan, we advise instructors to say certain things or ask certain questions. You should view these as suggestions, not mandates. If the natural progression of the conversation is moving to more in-depth questioning or conversation, by all means go with it. If you notice or hear something that you would like to elaborate on in the course of the lesson, take time to do that. Don't forsake powerful "a-ha" moments in service of the lesson plan. The lesson plan should be in service of those moments. Allow the lesson to go where it naturally progresses, skip sections where appropriate, add examples where necessary, and make it your own. You know your classroom and your students best, and we trust you to take the foundations of the lesson plans we've provided and build something truly powerful that will serve your students.

MINDSET BACKGROUND

In the early 1970s, psychologist Carol Dweck was studying how children responded to failure. Dweck and her research team devised an experiment involving difficult math problems that would allow them to gather data on how the children responded to failing a challenge. Dweck discovered that some students had a complete inability to cope with their failure. Other students approached the difficult task with the distinct attitude of wanting to learn from it and to challenge and grow their intellect. Dweck wondered what might cause these different reactions in children faced with challenges. This experiment was the beginning of Dweck's research into the mindsets.

Dweck coined the phrases "fixed mindset" and "growth mindset" to describe the way some students avoided challenges and others approached them head on. The fixed mindset is simply a belief that one's skills, abilities, and talents cannot be meaningfully developed. We sometimes refer to this as the "God-given talent" theory—the belief that you are born with only so much skill or ability in certain areas and there isn't much you can do to change that. According to this mindset, some people just have talent for things that others do not. Growth mindset, on the other hand, is the belief that with hard work, effort, and perseverance, one can develop their skills, talents, and abilities over time. Over decades of research, Dweck and her team amassed data that definitively showed that people who possessed a growth mindset had better outcomes in academics, careers, relationships, and other facets of life.

In *The Growth Mindset Coach* and *The Growth Mindset Playbook*, we outlined a series of steps teachers can take to create a growth-oriented classroom. A growth-oriented classroom focuses on growth over grades, progress over performance, and yet over right now. In this type of classroom environment, we reasoned, students' growth mindsets would have the best chance of flourishing.

In her TED Talk, "The Power of Believing You Can Improve," Dweck asks, "How are we raising our kids? Are we raising them for now instead of yet? Are we raising kids who are obsessed with getting A's? Are we raising kids who don't know how to dream big dreams? Their biggest goal is getting the next A or the next test score? And are they carrying this need for constant validation with them into their future lives?"

If we want to raise kids as Dweck described—for yet instead of right now, we must offer them spaces where they see the positive association between effort and growth. In a classroom, this begins with you, the teacher. No matter how much you teach and encourage growth mindset as a classroom teacher, you may be sabotaging it with your own fixed mindset. It is imperative that you approach each day, each interaction, with a growth mindset, always viewing your students and their potential through the lens of growth and modeling growth mindset daily.

Dweck writes in her book *Mindset*, "A person's true potential is unknown (and unknowable)... it's impossible to foresee what can be accomplished with years of passion, toil, and training." Stop viewing your students through the lens of your preconceived notions, instead approach each day with the belief that with hard work and perseverance your students—even the ones who struggle most—have the potential to achieve great things.

This belief will propel both you and your students to embark on the growth mindset journey. If students understand that you believe in their unlimited potential, it sets the stage for them to believe deeply in their own abilities. The goal of the growth mindset classroom is to develop in each student the love of learning. This is not an easy challenge. Students come to us with a range of obstacles. They may have learning disabilities, lagging skills in behavioral development, difficult home situations, trauma, chronic absenteeism, a lack of family support, or a variety of other challenges that may impact their availability for learning and academic performance at school. As teachers, we are responsible for seeing each student for who they are, to build relationships with them, and to set them up for success by helping them understand the connection between effort and improvement, regardless of circumstance.

TIPS FOR THE TEACHER

The objective of this book is to teach students about the power of growth mindset, the science of learning, and specific behavior and character strategies and skills that impact student success. As much as we have attempted to make these lessons suitable for any classroom, many of the activities skew younger. All of them, however, can be adapted to higher-level classrooms. Don't discount the power of Play-Doh and icebreakers in a high school classroom—we have used both to great effect. Prepare to adjust the lessons based on how your students respond to the learning and the tasks provided. We offer suggestions for doing this at the end of each lesson plan in the Supplemental/Extension Ideas section.

Although these lessons are meant to be taught in the span of 15 to 60 minutes, the objectives of the lesson should be revisited throughout the year. Teaching students about growth mindset and then abandoning the idea for the next several months will not help you make meaningful change in your classroom or in developing student skills. Be intentional about pointing out growth and fixed mindset messages and actions when you see them, continually discuss with students how their brains are doing the work of learning, and set up classroom practices that honor growth and progress over performance and perfect grades. These concepts need to be revisited often and become a part of your classroom ethos.

Beyond referring to the lesson objectives throughout the year, educators hoping to foster mindsets in the classroom can do other practices like the following:

> **Praise students for effort.** Replace phrases like "You're so smart" with comments about strategy or questions about effort. Emphasize the learning process in your praise. Say things like, "Wow, you did well on this test. How did you study for it?" Or, "I really like the way you took your time on your picture" instead of "You're so artistic!" Taking praise away from the person and instead emphasizing the process will go a long way in dismantling the belief that some people are just meant to be great at certain things, and building up the idea that with hard work and a good strategy anyone can be, do, and learn anything.

> **Normalize mistakes.** Mistakes can happen to anyone, especially when they are learning something new. Honor mistakes in your classroom as a normal and helpful part of the learning process. Find good work in mistakes where you can, and help students restrategize when something isn't working. A classroom where learning from mistakes is welcome fosters growth mindsets.

> **Create a culture of feedback in your classroom.** Teach your students to look at their work and others' work with a critical eye, and give them the language to give one another clear, strategy-focused feedback. A growth mindset classroom is a place where assignments can always be improved, projects can be revisited, and feedback is viewed not as a criticism, but as a path to deeper understanding.

> **Give parents the tools to promote a growth mindset at home.** Mindset is a fairly simple concept that any parent can incorporate into their home. Share research with them, teach them about the growth and fixed mindsets, and give them some strategies they can use at home to embrace challenges and apply a growth mindset.

In addition, educators will note that each section of this book embeds mindset and behavioral standards identified in "ASCA Mindsets and Behaviors for Students Success: K-12 College- and Career-Readiness for Every Student," from *Mindsets and Behaviors for Student Success: K-12 College- and Career-Readiness Standards for Every Student,* published by the American School Counselor Association. This book is a toolkit that focuses on the development of self-management, social skills, and learning strategies needed for encouraging grit and resilience in all students.

SECTION 1
ALL ABOUT
GROWTH MINDSET

"Success comes from knowing that you did your best to
become the best that you are capable of being."

—John Wooden

In this section, we'll focus on the concept of growth mindset and the science behind it. These lessons range from introductory vocabulary to critical thinking exercises that require examining our own experiences to see growth mindset at work in our lives. Once this foundational piece is in place, you can move on to subsequent sections that take a deeper dive into concepts, skills, and abilities essential to cultivating growth mindsets in your classroom.

LESSON 1
Mindset Assessment

Duration: 15–30 minutes

TEACHER TALK

We know what you're thinking—ugh. Another assessment? But do not fear, this super-simple, straight-forward mindset assessment has no right or wrong answers. You can (and should) take it right alongside your students. The purpose of this assessment is to gauge whether the test-taker leans toward a fixed or growth mindset in their overall attitudes and beliefs about learning. Use it as a foundational tool for examining the entrance into the mindsets. Once students (as well as colleagues, parents, and anyone else who wants to take the assessment) begin to understand their own beliefs about intelligence and how a fixed and growth mindset might influence achievement, you can begin the process of dismantling barriers to a growth-mindset environment and building practices that promote growth and improvement.

LEARNING OBJECTIVE

By the end of the lesson, students will be able to identify whether they tend toward a fixed or growth mindset.

RESOURCES AND MATERIALS

The resources and materials necessary to conduct this lesson are:

> Copies of the Mindset Assessment

> Growth Mindset and Fixed Mindset definitions

METHOD

> DO   Hand out a copy of the Mindset Assessment. Ask the students to put a check mark next to the statements they believe to be true. After all students have concluded the assessment, they will calculate how many odd-numbered statements had a check mark and how many even-numbered statements had a check mark. The odd-numbered statements represent fixed mindset thinking; the even-numbered statements represent growth-mindset thinking. If they have more of one than the other, it is likely they default to that mindset when dealing with life events and challenging situations. Share the definitions of growth and fixed mindset with students.

Growth mindset is the belief that intelligence and other qualities, abilities, and talents can be improved with effort, learning, and dedication over time.

Fixed mindset is the belief that intelligence and other qualities, abilities, and talents are fixed traits that cannot be significantly developed.

SAY   Research has shown that when students approach their school work and other pursuits with a growth mindset, they get better results. We will be talking a lot about growth mindset this year. I want you to have the ability to call on your growth mindset when you need it—like when you are taking on a hard challenge, solving a really difficult problem, or when you feel like you want to give up.

If your score leaned toward a fixed mindset, that's okay. We are all a mixture of fixed and growth mindsets. *(Here, you have an opportunity to share personal examples of situations in which a growth or fixed mindset impacted your outcome.)* But we're going to start practicing how to use our growth mindsets as we approach challenges and learning in our classroom, because I believe you can learn anything, and I want you to believe that too.

CHECK FOR UNDERSTANDING

Review the students' Mindset Assessments for completeness and accuracy of calculations. Check for understanding of fixed mindset and growth mindset definitions.

SUPPLEMENTAL/EXTENSION IDEAS

EXIT TICKET   Ask students for examples of when they had a growth mindset and/or a fixed mindset in their own lives.

WATCH   "Growth Mindset for Students (1 of 5)" by ClassDojo on YouTube

WATCH   "RSA Animate: How to Help Every Child Fulfill Their Potential" by The RSA on YouTube

DO   Have students take copies of the assessment to parents to start an at-home discussion.

MINDSET ASSESSMENT

Directions: Put a check mark next to all the statements you agree with.

_____ **1.** There are just some things I will never be good at.

_____ **2.** When I make a mistake, I try to learn from it.

_____ **3.** When others do better than me, I feel threatened.

_____ **4.** I enjoy getting out of my comfort zone.

_____ **5.** When I show others I'm smart or talented, I feel successful.

_____ **6.** I feel inspired by the success of others.

_____ **7.** I feel good when I can do something others cannot.

_____ **8.** It is possible to change how intelligent you are.

_____ **9.** You shouldn't have to try to be smart—you just are or you're not.

_____ **10.** I enjoy taking on a new challenge or task.

_____ **11.** If something is extremely difficult, it means it's probably not for me.

_____ **12.** When I fail at something, I usually just try again.

_____ **13.** Some people are just born good at some things, and that's okay.

_____ **14.** Anybody can improve if they put in the effort.

_____ **15.** It makes me feel good to show off what I'm good at.

_____ **16.** I like taking on a challenge.

_____ **17.** When someone criticizes me, I just ignore it.

_____ **18.** When someone criticizes me, I try to listen with an open mind.

_____ **19.** I don't like asking questions, because people might think I'm dumb.

_____ **20.** I am not afraid to ask questions about things I don't understand.

THE GROWTH MINDSET CLASSROOM-READY RESOURCE BOOK

GROWTH MINDSET

The belief that intelligence and other qualities, abilities, and talents can be improved with effort, learning, and dedication over time.

FIXED MINDSET

The belief that intelligence and other qualities, abilities, and talents are fixed traits that cannot be significantly developed.

LESSON 2
What Is Growth Mindset?

Duration: 40–60 minutes

TEACHER TALK

Teaching mindset begins with giving your students the vocabulary and understanding of the mindsets. When taught explicitly even the youngest learners can understand the differences between growth and fixed mindset. Beyond learning the textbook definition, it's also important that students are able to conceptualize growth and fixed mindsets at work in their own lives. Continued reflection on student beliefs about their ability to improve their intelligence, skills, and abilities is essential to cultivating growth mindsets in the classroom. Once you introduce the ideas of fixed and growth mindset, bring them into your daily teaching, discussion, and feedback as often as possible. This continued reference to the mindsets during authentic learning times will help your students cement the notion that their effort and perseverance have a direct impact on what they can achieve as learners.

LEARNING OBJECTIVE

By the end of the lesson, students will be able to define growth mindset and fixed mindset and provide examples of each.

RESOURCES AND MATERIALS

The resources and materials necessary to conduct this lesson are:

> Copies of My Fixed and Growth Mindsets

> Pencils or pens

> Nontoxic markers

> Growth Mindset and Fixed Mindset definitions

> White paper or white board

> T-Chart (Draw a T-Chart on a whiteboard or poster.)

> Projector

> Internet-enabled device

> YouTube access

METHOD

| DO | Activate prior knowledge by first asking students to fill out the first section of the My Fixed and Growth Mindsets. Have them write or draw about a time they tried really hard at something and got better. Then, ask students to think of a time when something felt hard and they gave up because they believed they could not get better. Ask students to write or draw about that experience.

Ask for volunteers to share their examples with the class. A Pair-Share would also be appropriate for sharing individual stories. Tell students that the examples they provided are examples of the fixed and growth mindsets.

Define growth mindset: Growth mindset is the belief that intelligence and other qualities, abilities, and talents can be improved with effort, learning, and dedication over time.

Define fixed mindset: Fixed mindset is the belief that intelligence and other qualities, abilities, and talents are fixed traits that cannot be significantly developed.

Read the following two stories to the students:

> When Jude joined the basketball team, he was excited, but at the first practice, Jude felt embarrassed that all the other players were better than him. He struggled to dribble the ball and his shots barely made it to the basket. His coach asked him to stay after practice to work on some shots, but Jude was tired and he thought it was unfair that no one else had to stay after, so he refused. At the team's first game, Jude sat on the bench for much of it and didn't score any points. After the game, he asked his mom if he could quit. When his parents asked why, Jude said he just wasn't cut out for basketball.

> When Erica joined the softball team, she was nervous. She had never played softball before but really wanted to try something new. At the first practice, she realized she had a lot of learning to do. Slowly, Erica learned the rules of the game, how to swing the bat, and how to throw. She often asked her dad to help her practice in the yard after dinner. During the first game, Erica struck out every time and missed two pop flies. She asked her dad to take her to the batting cages and she stayed after practice with the coach to practice fielding. During the last game of the season, Erica fielded two balls almost perfectly and hit a double that helped tie the game. She sat on the bench as well, and even though she knew she wasn't the best player on the team she was proud of herself for how much better she had become. She looked forward to joining the softball team again next year.

Now, make a T-Chart (see page 14). Ask students to examine the two stories and give examples of fixed and growth mindset. (*Examples of fixed Mindset: Jude quit the team, Jude wouldn't stay after with his coach, Jude was worried about the other players instead of himself. Examples of growth mindset: Erica practiced at home, Erica had a positive attitude, Erica stayed late to work on her skills, Erica didn't give up when she messed up.*)

"You Can Learn Anything" by Khan Academy on YouTube

SAY   In the video, it said that complex things are built on basic ideas that anyone can learn. Let's take a look at three people we are all familiar with and come up with ideas of things they had to learn first before they became great. (Make a list for each.)

Lebron James

Possible answers: He had to learn to dribble, shoot the ball, walk, run, etc.

Dr. Seuss

Possible answers: He had to learn to write, draw, invent rhymes, etc.

Beyoncé

Possible answers: She had to learn to read music, dance, hit musical notes, etc.

Note: You can substitute any recognizable personalities that may resonate with your students.

ASK   What do you think would have happened if LeBron James didn't score any points in his first game and quit? Or Beyoncé gave up because she lost a singing contest? Or someone told Dr. Seuss that his books were silly and no one would like them so he stopped writing altogether? *(Possible answers: LeBron wouldn't be one of the greatest players of all time; Beyoncé might not have pursued her dream to sing; Dr. Seuss wouldn't have published any books!)*

All people struggle before they stride, especially people who eventually become great. Growth mindset is believing you can do anything and working hard to get better. Fixed mindset is believing you can't get better and giving up.

CHECK FOR UNDERSTANDING

Determine whether or not students know the difference between the fixed and growth mindsets and are able to give real-world examples of each. Invite students to label their posters with the correct mindset and share how or why they made that determination.

SUPPLEMENTAL/EXTENSION IDEAS

DO   Post definitions of Growth Mindset and Fixed Mindset in your classroom for easy reference.

DO   Point to the fixed and growth mindset definitions when you see examples of each in your classroom.

WATCH   "The Power of Belief" TEDx Talk by Eduardo Briceño

WATCH   "The Power of Believing That You Can Improve" TEDx Talk by Carol Dweck

Write or draw about a time you tried really hard at something and got better:

Write or draw about a time something felt hard so you gave up:

Definitions to know:

Growth Mindset: The belief your skills, qualities, and abilities can improve with effort, hard work, and perseverance.

Fixed Mindset: The belief your skills, qualities, and abilities are fixed traits and cannot improve.

FIXED MINDSET EXAMPLES	GROWTH MINDSET EXAMPLES

THE GROWTH MINDSET CLASSROOM-READY RESOURCE BOOK

LESSON 3
Change My Words, Change My Mindset
Duration: 20–30 minutes

TEACHER TALK

So much of fostering a growth mindset in the classroom depends on how we speak to and communicate with our students. The purpose of this lesson is to help students understand that words have incredible power to propel us forward through a challenge or want to make us give up altogether. Changing our words to empower growth mindsets is one way to create a stronger classroom culture that values growth over grades and progress over perfection.

LEARNING OBJECTIVE

By the end of the lesson, students will be able to practice the skill of changing their words or self-talk to move from fixed-mindset language to growth-mindset language.

RESOURCES AND MATERIALS

The resources and materials necessary to conduct this lesson are:

> Growth and Fixed Mindset definitions

> Fixed Mindset Message Cards (Provide one set per group.)

> Pencils or pens

> Nontoxic markers

> Chart paper and/or whiteboard

METHOD

THINK, PAIR, SHARE | Think of a time that someone said something unkind to you. Turn to your partner and tell them what was said and how it made you feel. Take turns sharing your stories. Now, tell your partner about a time when someone said something kind to you and tell your partner how it made you feel. Take turns sharing your stories. (Optional: Have a few students share their personal story with the class or provide examples from literature.)

SAY | We know from the stories we shared that words have the power to make us feel really bad or really good. When someone says something hurtful or kind to us, we get different feelings. The same is true about the words we say to ourselves.

We have already learned what fixed and growth mindset are; here are the definitions to help you remember. (Use the Growth Mindset and Fixed Mindset definitions on page 9. Keep the definitions posted in your classroom for easy reference.)

Today, I am going to teach you a special trick to help you change your mindset with your words! Imagine you were trying to learn _____ *(substitute something you are learning in class)* and it was really difficult. You felt frustrated and angry and you believed you'd never get it. What kinds of things might you say to yourself when you are feeling that frustration? *(Examples: I quit. I don't want to do this anymore. This is stupid. I hate this. I can't get this. Record student answers.)*

When we say things like this, it's our fixed mindset talking. When we are in the fixed mindset, we want to take the easy way out because learning new things can be really difficult, and we don't want to look silly or not smart. But what's the problem when we give up trying to learn something just because it's hard? *(Possible answers: You'll never learn, you won't get better, you'll fall behind, etc.)*

Right! If we give up on ourselves, we'll never know how far we can really go. So I am going to share with you a strategy for changing your fixed mindset talk into growth mindset talk. Just like we can choose to say kind or unkind things to others, we can choose to say kind or unkind things to ourselves. Here's an example of something someone in a fixed mindset might say to themself: "I'll never be good at this."

How could we change that sentence into a growth mindset message? (Possible student answers: I might be good at this someday, I can get better at this if I try, I can do anything, etc.)

Sometimes changing the words we are saying to ourselves can make all the difference in our learning attitude. I'm going to hand out some cards with fixed mindset messages on them. On the back side of the card, I want you to rewrite a new growth mindset message. So, if one side of the card said, "I'll never be good at this," on the backside you might write: *(insert a student suggestion)*.

| DO | Have students work in pairs to rewrite the fixed-mindset messages on page 17. Move throughout the room to facilitate the activity; share student answers with the class periodically. Instill the power of the word "yet" when students struggle to reframe the fixed message.

CHECK FOR UNDERSTANDING

Listen to responses and check student understanding of growth-mindset messaging by reviewing the rewritten growth mindset messages on the backside of the cards. Take time to encourage students to practice using their growth mindset voices during tasks they may find difficult or challenging.

SUPPLEMENTAL/EXTENSION IDEAS

Create a "Change Your Words, Change Your Mindset" bulletin board featuring student examples.

| WATCH | "Removing Negative Self Talk" TEDx Talk by Abria Joseph

| READ | *Rosie Revere, Engineer* by Andrea Beaty

| LISTEN | "The Power of Yet: Official Music Video" by C. J. Luckey on YouTube

| WATCH | "Sesame Street: Janelle Monae—Power of Yet" by Sesame Street on YouTube

FIXED MINDSET

"I'll never be good at this."

FIXED MINDSET

"I made another mistake."

FIXED MINDSET

"This is too hard. I'm giving up."

FIXED MINDSET

"I tried, but I didn't do very well."

FIXED MINDSET

"I'm just not an artistic person."

FIXED MINDSET

"She'll always be better
at math than me."

FIXED MINDSET

"This assignment is
probably good enough."

FIXED MINDSET

"I don't want to ask questions;
I'll look stupid."

GROWTH MINDSET

GROWTH MINDSET

GROWTH MINDSET

GROWTH MINDSET

GROWTH MINDSET

GROWTH MINDSET

GROWTH MINDSET

GROWTH MINDSET

THE GROWTH MINDSET CLASSROOM-READY RESOURCE BOOK

LESSON 4
I Can Grow My Brain

Duration: 20–30 minutes

TEACHER TALK

You can help debunk the belief that some kids are just smarter, better at math, or more artistic by explicitly teaching students about neuroplasticity. Your students come to school each day with the goal of learning, but it's probably rare that they are taught how learning actually occurs in the body—the physiology behind the learning. This lesson is all about neuroplasticity. Neuroplasticity is a big, fancy word that just means that we can grow and shape our brains throughout our entire lives. Like plastic, our brains are malleable, and we can continue to learn new skills, make new connections, and improve our abilities our entire lives.

LEARNING OBJECTIVE

By the end of the lesson, students will be able to define neuroplasticity and how our brains can grow to learn new things.

RESOURCES AND MATERIALS

The resources and materials necessary to conduct this lesson are:

> White paper

> Pencils or pens

> How Did It Feel to Write with Your… T-Chart

> Building a Neural Pathway reflection sheet

METHOD

| SAY | I'd like you all to write the following sentence on the paper I handed out to you: I can learn anything. Now, I'd like you to switch to your nondominant hand and write the same sentence: I can learn anything.

| DO | Hand out the T-Chart (page 22) and have the students complete each side by asking the following questions:

> How did it feel to write with your dominant hand? Your nondominant hand?

> Why is writing one way easier than writing the other way? (*Possible answers: We practice, that's how we were born, etc.*)

SAY Writing with your dominant hand feels very easy because you have built neural pathways in your brain.

All of us are born with billions of neurons in our brains. These are tiny cells that communicate with each other to help us do things like write, move, speak, and think. In fact, neurons control everything that we do! The same neurons work together to complete the same tasks. So, when you are doing addition, a group of neurons work together to get the job done. But these neurons didn't know each other until you started to learn addition. As you were learning addition, the neurons sent messages to each other, and the messages created a pathway. The more you practiced addition, the faster and easier the messages traveled down the pathway. Also, just like exercise makes your body stronger, exercising your brain through learning and effort makes your brain grow stronger because you build more and faster neural pathways.

When you use your nondominant hand it is difficult and arduous because you haven't built a neural pathway yet. Now, let's try building the beginnings of a neural pathway. Write your name 10 times with your nondominant hand. What happens as you continue to write your name with your nondominant hand? *(Possible answers: It hurts my hand. I have to write slowly. It gets better the more I do it.)*

You can probably very quickly write your name with your dominant hand without thinking about it too much. But using your nondominant hand, the process is slow and you have to think about every pen stroke you make. When you do something fast without thinking too much about it, it's likely you've created a strong neural pathway. If you wrote with your nondominant hand all the time, you would eventually, over time, get really good at writing with your nondominant hand because you would develop a strong neural pathway.

Earlier you said that writing with your nondominant hand felt _____
(Insert student answers: hard, challenging, difficult, etc.). When you are engaging in something difficult and challenging and feel that sense of frustration, that is when you are building neural pathways and making your brain grow!

To extend this activity, I'm going to give you a take-home challenge. You are going to write down one thing you will work on really hard this week to grow a neural pathway. It has to be something that's difficult—something you aren't very good at yet. Then you'll report back your progress to see whether you were able to build a pathway.

DO Hand out the Building a Neural Pathway reflection sheet (page 23) to send home with students.

CHECK FOR UNDERSTANDING

Monitor progress on the neural pathway challenge, include what strategies students tried and whether or not they got better with effort. If a student indicates she did not get better at the task, help the student identify a new approach or strategy to try. Invite students to continue building new neural pathways by taking on challenging tasks. Think about how you can model developing a new neural pathway in your classroom in front of students. Let them observe you struggle, try new strategies, and improve. Don't forget to share your self-talk with students when you encounter a moment of frustration or success.

SUPPLEMENTAL/EXTENSION IDEAS

WATCH | "Neuroplasticity" by Sentis on YouTube

READ | *Your Fantastic, Elastic Brain: Stretch It, Shape It* by JoAnn Deak

READ | *The Brain That Changes Itself* by Norman Doidge

WATCH | "Your Brain Is Plastic" by SciShow on YouTube

HOW DID IT FEEL TO WRITE WITH YOUR...

DOMINANT HAND	NON-DOMINANT HAND

THE GROWTH MINDSET CLASSROOM-READY RESOURCE BOOK

BUILDING A NEURAL PATHWAY

Directions: Building a new neural pathway in your brain requires lots of practice. Think about one thing you'd like to get better at and spend this week practicing. Fill out this sheet as you go.

A new neural pathway I'd like to build is:

_____

_____

_____

_____

_____

Strategies I will use to build the pathway are:

_____

_____

_____

_____

_____

After working on building the pathway for one week, I noticed:

_____

_____

_____

_____

_____

LESSON 5
The Human Neuron

Duration: 30–60 minutes

TEACHER TALK

One of the most critical parts of teaching growth mindset to students is to give them information about how learning occurs in the body. Learning is just science and everybody has the potential to make connections for learning. Understanding how learning works in the body can bolster your growth mindset self-talk and messaging. When a student is struggling to learn a new concept you can say, "Oh, I see your neurons are trying to make a connection! Keep going!"

LEARNING OBJECTIVE

By the end of the lesson, students will be able to visualize how neurons within the brain work and the impact of fostering growth mindset messaging and self-talk.

RESOURCES AND MATERIALS

The resources and materials necessary to conduct this lesson are:

> Whiteboard or poster paper

> Nontoxic markers

> Copies of Meet the Neuron! worksheet

> Energy Stick or Sci-Fi Tube (These touch-activated energy tubes can be purchased on Amazon or at a local toy store. Some options include Steve Spangler's Energy Stick, WEY&FLY Sci-Fi Tube, or Toysmith Sci-Fi Tube. These are under $10 and you only need one to complete this lesson.)

METHOD

| SAY | Today, we're going to learn more about neurons. The neuron is one of the most interesting cells in the human body. All of you have billions of neurons in your body—if you didn't, you wouldn't be able to walk, talk, breath, or learn. We've already learned about neural pathways—the way our neurons connect to each other as we learn new things. Today, we're going to talk about the parts of the neuron and how those pathways are created in our bodies. Each of you has a neuron model, and we're going to label and annotate each part together.

As you look at the neuron model, imagine it as a tree. The cell body, or soma, is the trunk of the tree, the axon is the roots, and the dendrites are the branches. Draw the tree on a whiteboard or poster and label the parts. (Hand out Meet the Neuron worksheet, page 28.)

When a baby is born it has about one hundred billion neurons, but these neurons are not connected yet. Building connection between neurons is brain development in action. As you grow and learn, you create more and more connections between neurons.

Cell body or soma—The main body of the neuron, which contains its nucleus.

Dendrites—Extensions off the cell body (they look like branches); dendrites receive messages from other neurons.

Axon—The longest branch off the soma; the axon transmits electro-chemical signals to other neurons.

Myelin—Axons can be coated in myelin, a material that insulates the axon and makes communication with other neurons faster.

Axon terminal—The terminal is the end of the axon and is filled with neurotransmitters that can travel to other neurons.

We are going to create a neural pathway together!

| DO | Using nontoxic washable markers, have students label all the fingers on their right hand with "D" for dendrite, label their right hand with an "S" for soma, label their right and left arm with an "A" for axon (it's really long!), and label their left hand with "AT" for axon terminal. Have students label "N" on each of the fingers on their left hand for neurotransmitters. (You should label yourself, too! You'll be involved in the experiment!)

| SAY | You are now a neuron! The fingers on your right hand are dendrites; they receive messages. Your right hand is the soma, or cell body. This controls all the processes in your neuron. It is critical in sending and receiving messages. Your right arm and left arm are the axon. It's a really long branch off the soma, so we've made both of our arms the axon. Spread your arms wide to see how long it is! We've labeled our left hand with "AT" for axon terminal. When a message comes down the axon and reaches the axon terminal, chemicals called neurotransmitters are released. These neurotransmitters cross a small space called a synapse and connect with another neuron.

| DO | After the students have labeled the parts of the neuron cell on their body, assemble them into a large circle. They should not be touching but be very near each other.

| SAY | Look at the space between you and the people next to you. In the brain, this space is called a synapse. The neurotransmitters on your left hand have to cross the synapse to connect with the dendrites on the right hand of the person next to you. This is how we create neural connections!

I have this energy tube. It's going to represent a new skill that you have to learn. (*Indicate a new skill that students will be learning in your class.*) In order to learn this skill, you have to build a strong neural connection. We do this by creating neural connections in our brain. This tube uses human energy to light up. When it lights up, it means we've completed a connection.

Start by holding the tube in your left hand. Then, clasp the hand of the person to the left of you.

| DO | Do: Have each student, one by one, clasp the hand of the person next to them. When the person directly on your right clasps your hand, the connection is almost complete.

| SAY | We need to make the final circuit!

| DO | Have the student directly on your right clasp the other side of the energy tube. Once the circuit is complete, it will light up.

| SAY | We did it, we made a neural connection. So, what if somewhere along the way, we forget how to do something?

| DO | Instruct a student somewhere in the middle to unclasp hands. The tube will stop lighting up because the circuit has been broken.

| SAY | The more we do things, the stronger and faster these connections get. Instead of clasping hands one at a time, let's do it all at once as fast as we can. Ready? 1, 2, 3, go! (*The students clasp hands quickly and the tube lights up.*)

| DO | Try different ways to make the tube light up, representing learning.

Clasping hands very slowly	=	learning something for the first time
Breaking the connection somewhere	=	making a mistake or forgetting a step
Clasping hands very quickly	=	mastering the skill or concept
Small group	=	a simple skill
		(e.g., Start with a small group that represents learning a letter sound. Slowly add more students to the group to lengthen the connection. Say, "Here come more letter sounds, then sight words, then beginning readers, then picture books, then short novels, then full-size novels.")

CHECK FOR UNDERSTANDING

Listen for student feedback on applying growth mindset language during the different trials of making the tube light up. Model and foster corrections to any fixed messages. Invite students to come up with additional challenges to light the tube.

SUPPLEMENTAL/EXTENSION IDEAS

READ   *Your Fantastic Elastic Brain: Stretch It, Shape It* by JoAnn Deak

WATCH   "How Neurons Communicate" by BrainFacts.org on YouTube

MEET THE NEURON

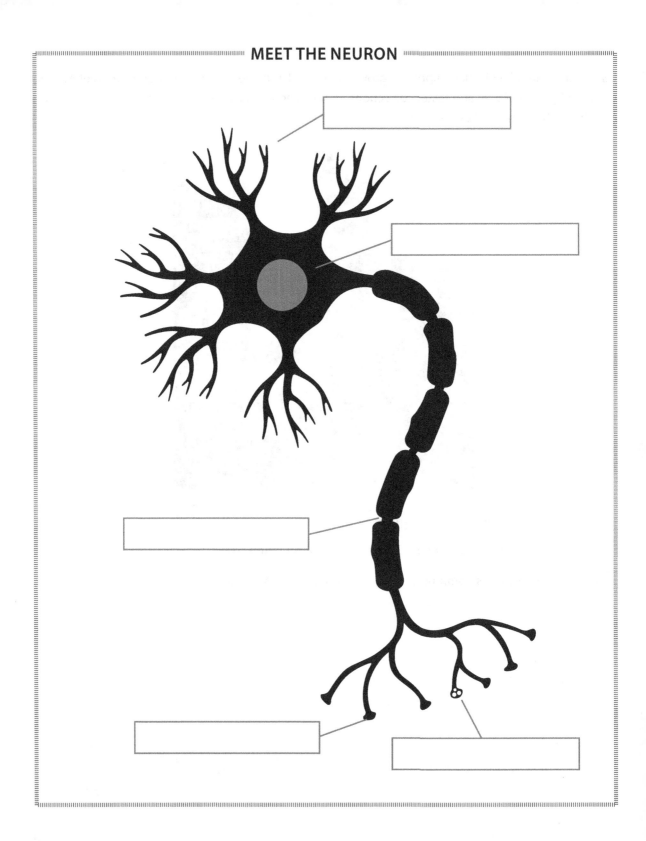

LESSON 6
Fixed Mindset Triggers

Duration: 40–60 minutes

TEACHER TALK

In her book, *Mindset,* Carol Dweck encourages us to recognize the environmental and internal triggers that lead to fixed-mindset thinking. Recognizing what your triggers are and having a plan to overcome those triggers and remain in your growth mindset are important skills. Before the lesson, think about what triggers your fixed mindset, such as an overbearing colleague, a pointless staff meeting, a challenging student, or a new initiative. Understanding the situations and feelings that lead us into a fixed mindset is the first step to controlling the situation. In this lesson, you'll help students understand what a fixed mindset trigger is, how to recognize their own triggers, and how to create a plan to help them avoid getting stuck in the fixed mindset.

LEARNING OBJECTIVE

By the end of the lesson, students will be able to identify what triggers their fixed mindset self-talk and how to adjust their thinking toward applying a growth-mindset self-talk.

RESOURCES AND MATERIALS

The resources and materials necessary to conduct this lesson are:

> Multiple task stations that may trigger fixed mindsets

> Copies of What I'm Thinking handout

> Highlighters

METHOD

| DO | Prior to the lesson, set up six task stations around the room that may "trigger" students to challenge their fixed mindset self-talk around the room.

| SAY | Today, we are going to talk about triggers. If something "triggers" you, what does that mean? *(Possible answers: It makes you angry, it makes you upset, etc.)* A trigger is an emotional response to a stimulus—like a song, event, or activity. Today, we're going to engage in a variety of different tasks and then talk about what we were thinking about when we were doing each task. You will record your self-talk on the What I'm Thinking handout (page 32) as you work through each task station.

Sample tasks:

> Solving a math problem

> Drawing a picture

> Creating origami

> Playing a new piece of music

> Learning a phrase in a new language

> Completing a Rubik's Cube

> Writing in calligraphy

> Doing a small puzzle

> Putting together a Lego kit

> Tying a shoe

> Solving a computer science task

> Labeling the parts of a plant, solar system, heart, map

> Sequencing words alphabetically or in another formula

> Building a structure such as a marble run or marshmallow and spaghetti tower

`DO` After the students have spent 3–5 minutes at each station, engaging in the task and recording their self-talk, reassemble the whole group and ask students to share what they encountered as they moved through each task. Debrief with the following questions:

> What was your self-talk and feelings toward each task?

> How did you respond to challenges?

> What stations or situations triggered your fixed mindset?

> What stations or situations encouraged your growth mindset?

Ask students to characterize their thought bubbles into fixed or growth messages—highlight fixed messages in one color and growth messages in another color.

CHECK FOR UNDERSTANDING

Listen to the discussions and responses and offer feedback for helping students recognize and respond to their fixed-mindset responses. Check student highlights to ensure understanding and provide feedback on the learning process.

SUPPLEMENTAL/EXTENSION IDEAS

| DO | Have students rewrite their fixed-mindset self-talk as growth-mindset self-talk.

| DO | Have students name their fixed mindset. Giving it a persona will help them better identify when it has been triggered. (Read *The Growth Mindset Coach* by Annie Brock and Heather Hundley for details on this lesson.)

WHAT I'M THINKING...

Directions: As you move through each task station, record your thoughts in the thought bubbles below.

Station 1

Station 2

Station 3

Station 4

Station 5

Station 6

THE GROWTH MINDSET CLASSROOM-READY RESOURCE BOOK

LESSON 7
The Self-Awareness Challenge

Duration: 60 minutes

TEACHER TALK

This lesson focuses on questioning students in a way that will lead them to identify their strengths and weaknesses and how they impact their work outcomes and relationships. This is key to developing a strong sense of self-awareness, or ability to reflect on their actions. Self-awareness is an important precursor to developing other social and emotional competencies like self-control, self-esteem, and self-efficacy. It plays an important role in how students learn and develop. Building self-awareness allows them to develop an understanding about their personal goals, how they feel, and why they are motivated to act in certain ways.

LEARNING OBJECTIVE

By the end of the lesson, students will be able understand the meaning of self-awareness and demonstrate knowledge of their individual strengths and weaknesses.

RESOURCES AND MATERIALS

The resources and materials necessary to conduct this lesson are:

> Self-Awareness definition

> Self-Awareness Task Cards 1–10

> Task Card Response Sheet

> Blank paper

> Colored pencils, crayons, and nontoxic markers

METHOD

| DO | Before the lesson, the teacher should watch "Self-Awareness" by ThinkTVPBS on YouTube to clarify the meaning of self-awareness and its connection to growth mindset.

| SAY | Today, we are going to talk about self-awareness. Self-awareness is understanding what you want, how you feel, and why you are motivated to act in certain ways. Self-awareness helps us reflect on our own actions. When we develop the ability to judge these things about ourselves it can help us consider the meaning of the behaviors and feelings of others as well, which can help us be a better friend and classmate. I'm going to read two situations to you and I want you to decide if the person in the story is demonstrating self-awareness.

Dante leaned across the aisle and flicked Kate with his eraser. Kate turned to Dante and asked him to please stop. Dante laughed and did it again. Kate scooted her desk away from Dante, but he leaned closer and flicked her again. "Please stop flicking me!" Kate said in a loud voice. The teacher heard the disturbance and came over to Kate. "Kate, what's wrong?" the teacher asked. "Dante is flicking me with his eraser and he won't stop." The teacher turned to Dante, who said, "It's not my fault Kate can't take a joke. I was just kidding around."

| ASK | Was Dante showing self-awareness in this story? How do you know?

| SAY | Now, let's try another story.

The day of the class presentations had arrived. Mia woke up covered in sweat and called for her mom. "Mom, I don't think I can go to school today," said Mia. "Why not? Do you not feel well?" her mother asked, feeling Mia's forehead for a temperature. "I'm not sick, but I'm so nervous. Today, I have to talk in front of the class for my presentation. I have butterflies in my stomach and I feel like I might throw up just thinking about it." It was clear to Mia's mom that she felt very uncomfortable talking in front of a crowd. "What's the worst that can happen?" asked Mia's mom gently. "Well, I could say the wrong thing and look stupid in front of the class," said Mia. "But," said Mia, "My partner Johan would have to do the presentation alone if I don't show up. Letting him down would feel worse than looking stupid. He'd be so upset." "Sounds to me like you have your answer. Get dressed, and I'll make your favorite breakfast," said Mia's mom. Mia got out of bed, told herself she could do this, and got ready to face the day.

| ASK | How did Mia show self-awareness in this story?

| DO | After students listen to the stories and have an understanding of self-awareness, draw their attention to the Self-Awareness Task Cards you have posted around the room. The task cards will be used as prompts to help students reflect on their own self-awareness. Students can complete responses to the task cards independently by writing and/or drawing their answers in the Task Card Response Sheet (page 37).

After visiting each of the task card stations, have students create a self-portrait on a blank sheet of paper. Have them label the drawing with their strengths and weaknesses using their answers to each of the task cards.

| SAY | Becoming self-aware starts with understanding our strengths and weaknesses. Next time, we're going to focus on our strengths and how we can use our strengths to help others and help make the classroom a better place. But, today, I want you to focus on those weaknesses and fears that you wrote down.

Improving your weaknesses and overcoming fears is to be aware of them—that's self-awareness. We're going to watch a video about how you can use self-awareness about weaknesses to change your strategy and improve your outcomes.

WATCH | "Self-Awareness" by LearningWorks for Kids on Vimeo

ASK | How did understanding weaknesses and changing strategy help the players in the video game?

SAY | Just like in the video, when we are aware of our weaknesses, we can make changes to our strategies to get a better outcome. If one of your weaknesses is listening to directions, you might change your strategy by taking notes during directions so you have them written down and can refer back to them. Being self-aware of strengths and weaknesses is an important first step to becoming an even better student and friend.

DO | Collect the sketches the students have completed for use in the next lesson.

CHECK FOR UNDERSTANDING

Review student work to monitor understanding of self-awareness. You will redistribute the drawings for Lesson 8 of this section.

SUPPLEMENTAL/EXTENSION IDEAS

READ | *The Lion Inside* by Rachel Bright and Jim Field

WATCH | "Minecraft Survival, Ep. 7: Self Awareness" by LW4K Let's Play on YouTube

SELF-AWARENESS TASK CARDS

Task Card 1: Identify your strengths at school.

Task Card 2: Identify your struggles at school.

Task Card 3: What do you enjoy doing at school? How do you feel when you are doing something you enjoy?

Task Card 4: What do you dread doing at school? How do you feel when you are doing something you don't enjoy?

Task Card 5: Name at least one thing you fear at school? Why do you fear this?

Task Card 6: Can you identify how to push past this fear? What would it take from you in order to do this? What might get in your way?

Task Card 7: What is the most harmful thing that may happen if you push past the fear? What is the best thing that may happen if you push past the fear?

Task Card 8: What regrets might you have if you don't push forward with overcoming the fear?

Task Card 9: Which area does your fear fall under?

1. Judgement from others

2. Not looking smart

3. The amount of effort you need to apply

4. The possibility of failing

5. The possibility of criticism

6. The threat of others who may already be successful.

7. Other _____

Task Card 10: List 3 things you would encourage someone else to do if they had this fear?

TASK CARD RESPONSE SHEET

Directions: Reproduce these task cards on card stock and distribute to each student.

What are your strengths at school?

What are your weaknesses at school?

**What do you enjoy about school? How do you feel when
you are doing something you enjoy?**

**What do you dread doing at school? How do you feel when
you are doing something you don't enjoy?**

Name at least one thing you fear at school. Why do you fear this?

Can you identify a way to push past the fear? What would it take
from you to do this? What might get in the way?

What is the most harmful thing that might happen if you pushed past the fear?
What is the best thing that could happen if you pushed past the fear?

What regrets might you have if you don't push forward with overcoming the fear?

THE GROWTH MINDSET CLASSROOM-READY RESOURCE BOOK

What area best describes your fear?

1. Judgment from others.

2. Not looking smart.

3. The amount of effort you need to apply.

4. The possibility of failing.

5. The possibility of being criticized.

6. The threat of others who may already be successful.

7. Other: _____

List three things you would tell someone who had your same fear.

1. _____

2. _____

3. _____

SELF-AWARENESS

Understanding what you want,
how you feel, and why you are
motivated to act in certain ways.

LESSON 8
The Chain of Strengths
Duration: 20–30 minutes

TEACHER TALK

Developing awareness of our strengths and how we can use them to help ourselves and others can create a powerful sense of positive interdependence in the classroom, fostering an atmosphere in which students rely on and encourage one another, where they are all on the same team, working to achieve both their independent and group goals.

In a culture of negative interdependence, fixed mindsets can flourish because students feel they have to best one another. In an environment of positive interdependence, the strengths of one contribute to the strength of the group. It is a value, not a threat. In this group-building activity, place a strong focus on the strength of each individual, calling special attention to how those individual strengths contribute to the overall group. Think of the *Avengers*: each superhero has his or her own strengths, but when they work as a team, they become unstoppable. Continue to foster an environment in which students are not competing against one another, but working together to improve individual outcomes and the outcomes of the group.

LEARNING OBJECTIVE

By the end of the lesson, students will be able to identify how their individual strengths can make the group stronger.

RESOURCES AND MATERIALS

The resources and materials necessary to conduct this lesson are:

> Strength and weakness self-portrait sketches from Lesson 7

> Copies of the Peer Feedback Interview sheet

> Construction paper

> Nontoxic markers

> Glue sticks

METHOD

 DO Remind students of the meaning of self-awareness and debrief them on the task featured in the previous lesson. Hand back their self-portrait sketches from the previous lesson and allow them to make any changes needed.

Group students into triads. Invite them to take turns sharing their sketches with the group, describing a couple of the strengths and weaknesses they listed. After each group member shares, have them fill out the Peer Feedback Interview sheet (page 42), asking their group for feedback.

It's critical for the classroom environment and student relationships to have a sense of safety, belonging, and support, otherwise sharing weaknesses will be counterintuitive. If safety and belonging are still in the developing phases in your classroom, you may need to refrain from putting students in a vulnerable situation by sharing out their weaknesses.

Have the students write down all their strengths on a strip of colorful construction paper. After writing down each strength on a strip of paper, the students will assemble a paper chain featuring all their strengths.

| SAY | This is our chain of strength! Chains are strong and flexible. We are also strong and flexible as a group. We are strong because each of us brings a different strength to this classroom. We are flexible because we can develop new strengths and use our strengths to help people when they need it. I'm going to hang our chain up in the classroom so we remember how strong we are when we all stick together. You are strong as individuals, but you are stronger together.

CHECK FOR UNDERSTANDING

Ask the students which would be more difficult to break in half, a single stick or a bundle of sticks? How could they compare this example to the strength of their team? Have students identify how and when they are stronger together. Listen to their answers and facilitate the discussion. Ensure all students see their value in this process. Ask how they can help each other continue to improve upon areas of weakness? Listen and respond by providing suggestions that will help students cultivate growth-mindset self-talk.

SUPPLEMENTAL/EXTENSION IDEAS

| DO | Have students continue to add links to the chain throughout the year as they develop new strengths.

| DO | Have students create a plan to improve areas they identified as weaknesses; check their progress throughout the year.

| WATCH | "A Pep Talk from Kid President to You" by SoulPancake on YouTube

| READ | *Not Your Typical Dragon* by Dan Bar-el

| DO | Have students take their self-portraits home and discuss strengths and weaknesses with their parents/family after Lesson 8 is completed.

PEER FEEDBACK INTERVIEW

Peer Feedback

How can my strengths help our team?

_____

_____

What is one idea for improving a weakness?

_____

Peer Feedback

How can my strengths help our team?

_____

_____

What is one idea for improving a weakness?

_____

Peer Feedback

How can my strengths help our team?

_____

_____

What is one idea for improving a weakness?

_____

LESSON 9
My Brain's Superpower: Neuroplasticity

Duration: 20–30 minutes

TEACHER TALK

The human brain is an incredible work of evolution. With every new experience and interaction with different environments, our brain changes as a response. Think of your brain as a computer, except instead of getting updates once a month, it's getting updates all the time. Neuroplasticity—the brain's ability to adapt throughout life—is happening all the time, but through practice, hard work, and effort, humans have the capacity to stimulate that change.

In this exercise, students will learn about their brains' ability to grow and change. For those who feel "stuck" with the brain they've got, good news! We have the power to encourage our brains to change and grow through our actions and habits.

LEARNING OBJECTIVE

By the end of the lesson, students will learn about neuroplasticity—the brain's ability to change and grow —and how this process plays a role in our lives.

RESOURCES AND MATERIALS

The resources and materials necessary to conduct this lesson are:

> Neuroplasticity definition card

> Computer and projector

> "The Backwards Brain Bicycle" by Smarter Every Day on YouTube

> Prism glasses (optional)

METHOD

| SAY | Today, we're going to learn a new word: neuroplasticity.

| DO | Write the word so students can see how it is spelled. Have students repeat the word, as necessary to achieve proper pronunciation.

| ASK | Did you know the human brain is wired for change?

| SAY | Even though our brains stop growing in size around the age of 25, it keeps changing our entire lives, thanks to a phenomenon known as "neuroplasticity." Neuroplasticity is our brain's ability to change and grow throughout our entire lives.

The word neuroplasticity is a combination of two words: neuron and plastic. Neurons are the billions of cells in our brains that connect together to help us do things. When neurons connect together, they create pathways in our brain. The more we use the new skill we learned, the quicker the neurons connect through the pathway. When you are really good at something, your neurons are firing superfast down the pathway you created. When you're not so good at something or just learning for the first time, the neurons are very slow. But the more you practice, the more your neurons remember and the faster the neurons get—that means you get faster and better at completing the task.

Now, here's the secret: Kids have a superpower when it comes to neuroplasticity. When you are young, your ability to learn new things is at its peak! Your brains are much more malleable than an adult's brain. We're going to watch a short video about neuroplasticity.

| WATCH | "The Backwards Brain Bicycle" by Smarter Every Day on YouTube.

| SAY | In the video, it took Destin, the adult, eight months to learn how to ride the backward bicycle, but it only took his young son two weeks. That's because children's brains are even more malleable than adults'—you have the power of neuroplasticity!

Optional discussion: Tell a story about a time you had to work really hard to improve at a skill, and make connections to "The Backwards Brain Bicycle," including the process you went through to get better.

Optional activity: Purchase "prism" glasses or alter standard safety goggles with stick-on prisms, and have students toss a ball into a bucket without the glasses on and then with the glasses on. Note how easy it is to toss the ball when the students are not wearing the glasses—they have trained their brain to toss a ball this way. When they put on the glasses it's a totally new experience. At first, tossing the ball will be very difficult with the glasses on, but as their brains adjust to the new glasses, it becomes easier. Have students discuss the changes and note how many tosses it takes to get better with the glasses. Then have students remove the glasses and go back to tossing without them. Note what it feels like to adjust to the "normal" way of tossing the ball.

CHECK FOR UNDERSTANDING

Listen to student discussions on neuroplasticity. Encourage them to make a plan to learn something new, to challenge a parent to do the same, and to teach others about their superpower. Provide opportunities for them to go to other classrooms and share their understanding of their superpower. Some ideas to try include:

> Learning to juggle

> Learning a new language

> Playing an instrument

> Learning a new dance routine

> Learning a handshake

> Learning to ride a unicycle

SUPPLEMENTAL/EXTENSION IDEAS

| DO | Follow the instructions on "How Your Brain Works for Kids: Growth Mindset and Neuroplasticity" by I HAVE A GO on YouTube to build a brain.

| SING | "Neuron Song: Growth Mindset and Neuroplasticity for Kids" by I HAVE A GO on YouTube

| READ | *Neurocomic* by Dr. Hana Roš and Dr. Matteo Farinella

| WATCH | "After Watching This, Your Brain Will Not Be the Same" TEDx Talk by Lara Boyd (for older students)

| READ | "Neuroplasticity: Learning Physically Changes the Brain" by Sara Bernard on Edutopia.org

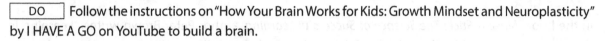

NEUROPLASTICITY

The brain's ability to adapt and form new neural connections throughout our lives.

LESSON 10
How to Train Your Brain

Duration: 20–30 minutes

TEACHER TALK

In the book, *Make It Stick: The Science of Successful Learning*, author Peter Brown writes, "Learning is deeper and more durable when it's effortful. Learning that's easy is like writing in sand, here today and gone tomorrow." Brown goes on to detail how using retrieval practice and other intentional learning strategies can be far more powerful than rereading, highlighting, using flash cards, or cramming the night before a test—you know, the typical ways our students usually study. By giving students simple strategies to improve their study habits, we have the power to help them retain information for long periods of time and use the things we teach them today throughout their lifetimes.

LEARNING OBJECTIVE

By the end of the lesson, students will be able to practice strategies for retrieving information in class or independently.

RESOURCES AND MATERIALS

The resources and materials necessary to conduct this lesson are:

> Copies of My Question Map

> Copies of Retrieval Practice Tic-Tac-Toe board

> Copies of Retrieval Practice Exit Tickets

METHOD

Embedding retrieval practice into your lessons is greatly beneficial to student learning. Explicitly teaching students how to use the practices on their own is a skill that will serve them well as they learn new material.

Strategies for retrieval practice that students can utilize:

> Record one question they have about the learning and two things they learned during any given lesson. Encourage students to share in think, pair, share groups and provide feedback to students.

OR

> Invite students to record information in question maps using prompts to help guide the retrieval process and adding other information they may recall.

DO After a lesson, have partners or triads work through a "brain dump" by writing down all the information they can recall from the lesson or by creating and distributing My Question Map (page 50), in which all students start with a big question about the lesson, and then ask more questions that come to mind. Students can use their papers to formulate questions for a game of Retrieval Tic-Tac-Toe.

Pass out a Retrieval Practice Tic-Tac-Toe grids (page 48) to be shared between teams, or you can divide your class into two teams and display a large tic-tac toe board on a poster or whiteboard.

> Students should use their brain dump notes or their My Question Map worksheets to formulate questions for the opposing team to answer. They should determine who will be X's and O's on the board.

> One team will ask a question while the other team collaborates to come up with the correct answer. If the team has the correct response they can place the predetermined X or O on the board.

> The teams will take turns asking and answering questions and adding the corresponding X or O to the board until the game is complete.

> The teacher can utilize this as a formative check by facilitating around the room to check for correct responses, misconceptions, and unclear learning. Use the information gleaned from the task to adjust instruction in order to meet the needs of the learners.

CHECK FOR UNDERSTANDING

Observe students utilizing retrieval practice strategies in their learning and encourage them to continue to practice these tasks on their own. Incorporating quizzes intermittently throughout your lessons will help students in deliberately retrieving information. Remember, there is a difference between practicing to retrieve information and summative testing. Retrieval practice is part of the learning process, and grades should not be given. Instead, provide meaningful feedback to your students based on the formative check.

SUPPLEMENTAL/EXTENSION IDEAS

DO Provide students with additional tools to practice retrieving information. Have them create their own flash cards and practice effectively using them. Have them add sketches or drawings to notes or use concept maps, question maps, and other graphic organizers. Don't forget that summarizing the learning is an important step as well. Incorporating clickers, exit tickets, and writing prompts are effective practices to increase retrieval practices in learning.

DO Visit retrievalpractice.org for more information and free resources.

WATCH "Study Strategies: Retrieval Practice" by The Learning Scientists on YouTube

RETRIEVAL PRACTICE TIC-TAC-TOE

RETRIEVAL PRACTICE EXIT TICKETS

Exit Ticket

Two things I learned are:

_____

_____

One question I have is:

_____

_____

Exit Ticket

Two things I learned are:

_____

_____

One question I have is:

_____

_____

Exit Ticket

Two things I learned are:

_____

_____

One question I have is:

_____

_____

MY QUESTION MAP

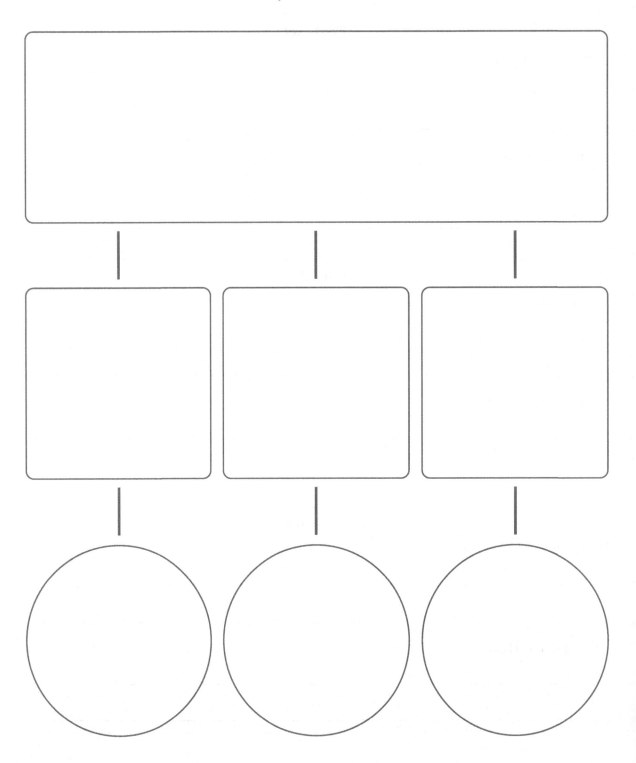

SECTION 2
BUILDING OUR CLASSROOM COMMUNITY

"Alone we can do so little, together we can do so much."

—Helen Keller

In this section, we'll be building a community classroom of learners. Setting classroom norms and rules are a typical part of any classroom, but what if you set those norms through the lens of a growth mindset? This small change in the rules, agreements, routines, and ethos you adopt together as a learning community can help you nurture a growth mindset in students—students who understand the value of individual effort, as well as collective efficacy.

LESSON 1
Setting Classroom Norms

Duration: 20–30 minutes

TEACHER TALK

Teachers often set classroom norms on the first day of school, but this can be counterintuitive. Learning what norms are necessary for your particular group of students takes time. Waiting to establish norms will help you determine areas your class will need to spend time developing. This wait time will also help you to be more intentional on teaching and monitoring practices that help students develop the growth-mindset language.

In this lesson, you'll be asked to do some observation work in the weeks leading up to setting classroom norms. This will help you convey to the students the problem areas you have identified and enlist their help in finding solutions through the establishment of classroom norms.

Be aware of the difference between "rules" and "norms." Rules are meant to be obeyed, usually in service of student safety, and come from the teacher. A rule might be, "Ask before you leave the classroom." This rule can and should be established on day one. A "norm," on the other hand, is a collective decision, agreed upon by all members of the group. When students are involved in the process of formulating the classroom norms, they will be more likely to follow and enforce them because they have a personal investment.

LEARNING OBJECTIVE

By the end of the lesson, students will be able to work together to create classroom norms that support a growth-oriented learning environment in which they have a sense of safety, support, and belonging. It is necessary to create and cultivate this ethos so students feel more comfortable to take risks, reduce judgement of one another and themselves, and develop their skills, talents, and abilities in a growth-oriented environment.

RESOURCES AND MATERIALS

The resources and materials necessary to conduct this lesson include the following:

> Discussion questions

> T-Chart (see example below)

> Sticky notes

METHOD

| DO | Pose questions based on two to four weeks' worth of observations in your classroom prior to setting classroom norms. List the questions or problems you have observed on one side of a T-Chart. Ask students to respond on their sticky note with potential answers that could be used to establish a norm to combat the problem. (See the example provided for clarity.)

Use student responses to help discuss and organize five to seven class norms that will promote and support a growth environment for all students. Reword the norms using positive and simple language for easy reference. You may even consider summarizing the norms into one or two "power words" that will help them to be easily referenced and enforced.

Observation/Problem	Solution
Observation: When we get ready to complete independent work, I hear students say "she must be really smart because she gets her work done quickly." **Why is it a problem?** This makes students worried about not looking smart if they need to take more time to complete the assignment.	**Possible Solution:** Speed/timed tests should not be used to determine if someone is smart or not. Consider giving behavior-specific praise to those who are diligent in completing work accurately rather than fast.
Observation: Students have been observed not asking questions and using limited strategies for solving problems. Students don't ask questions because others laugh if they are incorrect or make a mistake **Why is it a problem?** We limit our learning when we don't ask questions and mistakes are part of the learning process. We will not be able to grow as problem solvers if we don't ask questions and nor will we grow our brains if we don't embrace mistakes as part of our learning.	**Possible Solution:** Encourage students to try a variety of strategies and to work as problem solvers. Promoting a collaborative learning environment will set the tone for this process. Invite students to review their mistakes and to evaluate how and why the mistake was made. Teach students how to respond to peers who make mistakes and alter fixed self-talk when they make mistakes.

POSSIBLE CLASSROOM NORMS TO ESTABLISH:

Use behavior specific praise and process feedback with growth language.

"I really like how you focused on getting the task done by staying at your center and showing your work as well as trying new strategies."

Be a problem solver

Examples of Power Word(s):

> Growth-Focused

> Problem Solver or Resourceful

CHECK FOR UNDERSTANDING

Post the norms in the classroom. Add actions to each norm, along with a non-linguistic representation, and teach how to properly respond when the norm is not practiced. Remind students of the classroom norms by making it part of the daily routine; this will help to reinforce your desire to create a learning environment conducive to encouraging all learners to develop and apply a growth mindset. Don't forget to respond to missteps by using growth-oriented language.

SUPPLEMENTAL/EXTENSION IDEAS

| DO | Have students describe or journal about their learning each day based on the Power Words that summarize the norms. *(Example: I was a problem solver when I used my resources (notes, books, peers, visuals) to help me work through a task.)*

OUR CLASSROOM NORMS

1. _____

_____

_____

2. _____

_____

_____

_____

3. _____

_____

_____

_____

4. _____

_____

_____

_____

5. _____

_____

_____

_____

LESSON 2
Developing Emotional Intelligence

Duration: 20– 30 minutes

TEACHER TALK

Emotional intelligence is a critical part of effective communication with others, and research has indicated that it plays a role in student achievement. In this lesson, we will be examining different types of emotions and how we can use our understanding of our own emotions to better communicate with others. Using examples from your personal experience—whether you were in control of your emotions or you failed to be in control of them—can provide a powerful model for students as they begin to understand their own emotional responses to situations. Don't be afraid to talk about these experiences in your own life! Your candor will serve to help students be more honest with themselves and others about their emotions and develop emotional intelligence.

LEARNING OBJECTIVE

By the end of the lesson, students will be able to identify what emotional intelligence is and how we can use our understanding of emotions to connect with others and respond to situations in a more mindful and self-regulated capacity.

RESOURCES AND MATERIALS

> "Meet Riley's Emotions," a clip from Pixar's *Inside Out*. (This clip can be taken from the movie, or find the clip on the Stuffs That Matters channel on YouTube.)

> Emotional Intelligence definition

> Printout of Snow Day! An Emotional Intelligence Activity

> Copies of Snow Day Response Sheet

METHOD

| SAY | We've been talking about growth mindset—the belief that you can get better at anything with hard work and effort. Today, we are going to talk about feelings we might encounter as we try to get better at something. Psychologist Paul Eckman identified the six basic human emotions as anger, fear, sadness, disgust, joy, and surprise. We are going to study five emotions based on the movie *Inside Out*. First, I'm going to show you a short clip from the film.

| WATCH | "Meet Riley's Emotions" by Stuffs That Matters on YouTube

| SAY | *(after watching the clip)* In this clip, we met Joy, Anger, Fear, Sadness, and Disgust. We all have these emotions!

Today, we're going to talk about emotional intelligence. Let's break that down into two parts: emotion and intelligence.

| ASK | What does being intelligent mean? *(Possible answers: being smart, knowing things, etc.)* Right, being intelligent means having a strong understanding of or knowledge about something. What does emotion mean? *(Possible answers: feelings, etc.)* Yes, an emotion is a strong feeling—it can be a feeling of happiness, anger, fear, sadness, or disgust. Those are all emotions. When we combine the two, we get emotional intelligence. What do you think that means? *(Possible answers: being smart about your feelings, etc.)* Yes, having emotional intelligence means that you can understand your own feelings and the feelings of others.

| DO | Post the definition of emotional intelligence for easy reference.

| SAY | The first thing to understand is that not all people have the same emotional response to a situation. So, we are going to play a game called Snow Day! I have set up six stations around the room showing different people who are affected by a snow day in different ways. Your job is to record the emotions those people might be feeling about the snow day on your recording sheet.

| DO | Ask students to debrief in small groups or as a class on each person affected by the snow day. Facilitate discussion about how different people have different emotions, even about the exact same event.

For older students, create characters for a situation that requires them to think more critically about emotional responses. For example, someone posted the answers to Mr. Wilson's test online the day before the exam. How might various people feel about this?

CHECK FOR UNDERSTANDING

Review student responses to check on how they connected an emotion to each task. Gather student rationale for clarification and expand upon building emotional intelligence by applying the learning to daily lesson opportunities.

SUPPLEMENTAL/ EXTENSION IDEAS

| LISTEN | Have students make an emotions playlist with songs that represent each of the five emotions discussed.

| DO | Ask students to find synonyms for each of the five emotions.

| DO | Ask students to combine emotions to see how they work together (e.g. Fear + Anger = Hatred, Sadness + Fear = Anxiety, etc.).

EMOTIONAL INTELLIGENCE
The ability to understand your own emotions and the emotions of others.

SNOW DAY!
An Emotional Intelligence Activity
A blizzard hit the down on Friday. All schools have been closed. It's a snow day!

DEREK
Third Grader
Derek has been nervous about the spelling test on Friday. He didn't study as much as he should have. He just needs a little more time to get ready for the test.

MR. JOLSON
Classroom Teacher
Mr. Jolson worked hard to arrange a special guest speaker to come to his class Friday. After Friday, the speaker will be traveling overseas and unable to visit the class any other day.

MRS. SMITH
School Principal
Mrs. Smith has to drive to school on Friday, even though school has been canceled. She needs to make sure no kids are accidentally dropped off and arrange for custodians to shovel the sidewalks.

MING
Fifth Grader
There is nothing in the world Ming loves more than sledding. Ming has been hoping for a big snow so she and her friends could sled down the big hill at the park.

SERENA
First Grader
Friday was the school talent show audition. Serena was performing a piece on the piano for the show. She has been practicing for weeks, and she's so excited to do the audition.

OFFICER ROGERS
Local Police Officer
This blizzard is making driving conditions very difficult. Officer Rogers has been called out on duty to patrol the streets and help people who might wreck their car or slip and fall in the snowy conditions.

SNOW DAY RESPONSE SHEET

Directions: Read the snow day situations for each person. Write down your response about you think they might feel about the snow day.

How is Derek feeling? _____

_____

_____

How is Mrs. Smith feeling?

_____

_____

How is Serena feeling?

_____

_____

How is Mr. Jolson feeling?

_____

_____

How is Officer Rogers feeling?

_____

_____

How would YOU feel?

_____

_____

WHAT I'M THINKING...

Directions: As you move through each task station, record your thoughts in the thought bubbles below.

Station 1

Station 2

Station 3

Station 4

Station 5

Station 6

LESSON 3
An Attitude of Gratitude—Pay It Forward
Duration: 20–30 minutes

TEACHER TALK

When we give or receive gratitude, our brain gets a boost! Research has shown that when we express or receive thanks, our brains release dopamine and serotonin, two feel-good chemicals that can make us feel happier. Gratitude doesn't have to be spontaneous. Intentional expressions of gratitude can have the same effects on our mood. In this lesson, you'll help students understand what gratitude is and set up an intentional gratitude practice in your classroom.

LEARNING OBJECTIVE

By the end of the lesson, students will be able to identify what they are grateful for and understand how practicing gratitude can support happiness and foster growth.

RESOURCES AND MATERIALS

> Gratitude definition sheet

> Copies of Gratitude Cards

METHOD

| DO | Post the definition of gratitude on a word wall. Share with students that gratitude is a state of mind and the expression of being thankful and appreciative.

| SAY | Practicing gratitude has been proven to increase happiness and overall well-being, and is even beneficial when taking on challenging tasks and persevering through adversity. When you express your gratitude, your brain releases dopamine and serotonin, which are responsible for helping you feel happy. Practicing gratitude daily will strengthen neural pathways, thereby enhancing the feeling of happiness.

Turn to a partner and talk about three things you are grateful for; then switch roles and have your partner share three things they are grateful for.

| DO | Have students share one thing their partner is grateful for and record the responses where students can view them.

Add time each day for gratitude practice. This can be done easily by adding the dry erase gratitude desk prompt for expressing gratitude. In addition, it is important to foster practicing gratitude when students face adversity or a challenge, or are feeling stressed.

To make the dry erase gratitude desk prompt, reproduce and laminate the dry erase "desk prompt" for students to use to practice gratitude daily, or print and place the desk prompt in a page protector for them to record their responses.

CHECK FOR UNDERSTANDING

Encourage students to practice gratitude in an effort to build stronger neural pathway connections and to boost happiness. Huddle up each week to foster an attitude of gratitude as a class. You can review student desk prompts to gather insight into student understanding.

SUPPLEMENTAL/EXTENSION IDEAS

| READ | *Bear Says Thanks* by Karma Wilson |

| READ | *Sylvester and the Magic Pebble* by William Steig |

| READ | *Thanks a Million* by Nikki Grimes |

| READ | *The Thankful Book* by Todd Parr |

| WATCH | "Want to Be Happy? Be Grateful" TED Talk by David Steindl-Rast |

GRATITUDE

The quality of being thankful; readiness to show appreciation for and to return kindness.

Directions: Reproduce, laminate, and distribute the cards to students.

GRATITUDE CARD

I have gratitude for:

1._____

2._____

3._____

GRATITUDE CARD

I have gratitude for:

1._____

2._____

3._____

GRATITUDE CARD

I have gratitude for:

1._____

2._____

3._____

GRATITUDE CARD

I have gratitude for:

1._____

2._____

3._____

LESSON 4
My Core Values

Duration: 20–30 minutes

TEACHER TALK

Before we begin this lesson, we must ask ourselves: What are values? Values are the things you think are important in yourself and in others. They are the guiding principles of our lives. Our values impact our decisions and actions daily. An individual often has a range of values, and what is valuable to one person may not be valuable to another.

Identifying our core values not only helps us prioritize events in our lives, but they shape who we choose to build relationships with. Think about your list of core values before beginning this lesson. Remember, you can have many values, but try to shrink your list to three that are of the highest priority for you. Once we identify our values, we can compare them to the choices we make daily and evaluate whether or not we are living our most important values.

LEARNING OBJECTIVE

By the end of the lesson, students will be able to identify three personal core values and three qualities they value in others as well as why they are important.

RESOURCES AND MATERIALS

> Definition of Core Value

> Copies of the Tri-Fold Instructions

METHOD

| DO | Share with students that core values are guideposts that assist us in our thinking and actions. They help us maintain focus, provide clarity toward a purpose, and help to determine intent.

| ASK | What kind of person do you want to be and why? What matters to you the most and why?

| DO | Distribute a copy of the Tri-Fold Have Instructions to each student and have them record three personal core values on the left flap of the tri-fold. Under each flap, have them record why those values matter to them. On the right flap, have students write three qualities they value in others. Under each flap, have them identify why those qualities are important for their friend to have.

On the center of the tri-fold, ask students to follow about one of the prompts below.

> Create a Venn diagram and compare similarities and differences in the values you listed.

> What do you feel is the most important value and why?

> Who is a person you admire that has the value you find to be most important? How does that person behave?

> Share what is the same or different between your personal core values and what you value in others.

> How do your values help you to make decisions?

> Do your values enhance the growth messaging within the classroom? Explain. If not, what impact do you think your value(s) will have on the classroom environment?

> Do you have a value that you feel you need to improve? Provide an example of why you want to continue to practice improving on this value and how you plan to do so.

Once the task is complete, encourage students to share with partners or small groups what they have learned about themselves and how their values contribute to the classroom environment.

CHECK FOR UNDERSTANDING

Listen to the discussions and review the tri-folds to determine if students have grasped an understanding of how their values can help guide how they make decisions. Create a class list of the values students shared on their tri-folds and help provide guidance when students steer off course or need help navigating challenging situations with peers. Recalling our core values helps us refine our own actions and understand the angle in which others make their decisions.

SUPPLEMENTAL/EXTENSION IDEAS

Present multiple scenarios or Aesop fables and have students evaluate the values of the characters using the questions below. (Aesop fables are available for free in the Library of Congress online database.)

| READ | Aesop Fable: *Lion and the Mouse*

| READ | Aesop Fable: *The Tortoise and the Hare*

| READ | Aesop Fable: *The Boy Who Cried Wolf*

| READ | Aesop Fable: *The North Wind and the Sun*

> How do these values set purpose?

> Do the values align with yours? Why or why not?

> How would you encourage someone who lost their focus? Provide examples of how to support that person. How can we use our core values to set the tone for using growth-mindset messaging and practices?

| DO | Have students write a reflection of a time they did not stay true to their values and the impact that experience had and what they learned from the experience.

CORE VALUES

The guideposts that assist us in our thinking and actions. They help us maintain focus, provide clarity toward a purpose, and help to determine intent.

TRI-FOLD INSTRUCTIONS

LESSON 5
Developing Empathy

Duration: 20–30 minutes

TEACHER TALK

The concept of empathy is simple. It's the ability to identify with another person's feelings, point of view, or experience, to put yourself in their shoes, so to speak. But empathy in practice can be difficult to do. Humans are inherently egocentric. After all, we play the starring role, complete with mental narration, in every experience and interaction of our lives.

Empathy is a skill that can be practiced and developed. Teaching students to be conscious about the feelings of others through the practice of empathy can create a more respectful and safer environment—an environment in which students are not scared to try new things, ask when they need help, or move beyond their comfort zones.

LEARNING OBJECTIVE

By the end of the lesson, students will be able to distinguish the difference between sympathy and empathy and understand how to be an empathic friend.

RESOURCES AND MATERIALS

The resources and materials necessary to conduct this lesson are:

> Expression scale (page 70)

> Book: *Hey, Little Ant* by Phillip and Hannah Hoose

METHOD

| SAY | Empathy means connecting with others and feeling what they feel without judging them. It is putting yourself in another person's shoes and trying to see things from their point of view.

| DO | Share the expression scale with students and explicitly help them identify how the facial expressions on the scale relate to feelings. Ask students to share with a partner a time when they could identify with one of the expressions and its representative feelings. Share stories and model empathic responses to their stories.

Next, play a game called "What's My Face?"

Students stand in a circle and look at the floor. A student begins the game by thinking of an emotion and making a face to match the emotion. This student will then tap the person next to them on the shoulder. When the second player looks up at the first player, they will share the face. The second player will pass the expression on to the next player by tapping them on the shoulder and sharing the face. The expression is passed around the circle. Once everyone has had a chance to pass the face, the first player will say "What's my Face?" The players then share and discuss the feelings associated with it.

READ Hey, Little Ant by Phillip and Hannah Hoose. In the story, a boy attempts to squish an ant in an effort to impress his friends, but when the ant starts speaking to him, he learns a valuable lesson on empathy and perspective taking. While reading, stop and ask students to identify with the boy and the ant by naming and defining their feelings. Encourage the students to use the expression scale and share how the boy and ant might feel in the story. Ask students to write or draw a new ending to the story that demonstrates what they have learned about empathy.

CHECK FOR UNDERSTANDING

Check student-created endings to Hey, Little Ant to see that they have demonstrated an understanding of empathy.

Ask students the following prompts:

> How do you know when someone is being empathetic?

> What behaviors, actions, or words are shown or expressed when someone is being empathetic?

> Describe, write, or draw ways to show empathy.

You can share empathetic prompts with students who are practicing showing empathy. Recognize acts of empathetic listening and response when demonstrated by students. Read additional stories and encourage students to discuss if the character(s) expressed empathy.

SUPPLEMENTAL/EXTENSION IDEAS

READ You, Me, and Empathy by Jayneen Sanders

READ I Am Human: A Book of Empathy by Susan Verde

READ Last Stop on Market Street by Matt de la Peña

READ Adrian Simcox Does NOT Have a Horse by Marcy Campbell

WATCH "Brené Brown on Empathy" by The RSA on YouTube

DO Have students develop a class social story on empathy, or role-play what it looks like and sounds to be empathic.

DO Take pictures of students acting out different situations, and have the students write empathetic captions or a script. For example, students can pose in pictures that demonstrate a student has fallen and scraped his or her knee, has done poorly on an assignment, loses a toy at recess, has a friend move away, etc.

EXPRESSION SCALE

THE GROWTH MINDSET CLASSROOM-READY RESOURCE BOOK

SECTION 3

CHALLENGING OURSELVES; GROWING OURSELVES

"Satisfaction lies in the effort, not in the attainment; full effort is full victory."

—Mahatma Gandhi

In this section, we will be focusing on the value of digging into challenges. Many students, particularly those operating in the fixed mindset, shy away from challenges because they are afraid to fail. But we know that failure is actually our friend! Encountering challenges and learning how to use effort and strategy to overcome it are key pieces of the mindset puzzle. Here we'll take a deep dive into the value of challenge and help you create environments in your classroom in which students can practice grappling with a difficult challenge.

LESSON 1
Trial and Error: A Resilience Strategy

Duration: 60–90 minutes or two 45-minute lessons

TEACHER TALK

Resilience is the ability to bounce back after failure. When we experience failure or difficulty, our body goes into a "fight, flight, or freeze" mode. The stress response created by failure is enough to make some people stop dead in their tracks and run from the problem. But people who have developed a healthy resilience to challenges have the capacity to restrategize and recover from failure. Resiliency isn't reserved for the few who are born with it, it's a skill that can be developed with the right strategies and attitude.

There are a few crucial things you can do to build resilience in your classroom. First, always model resilience. If a lesson plan doesn't go the way you would have liked or a field trip gets canceled, talk through the process. Model the art of reframing the situation, or finding another strategy or approach to the challenge. Next, let kids grapple with difficulty and failure. Our natural inclination might be to help them solve the problem, but resist the urge. If they come to you with a problem, focus on asking questions to help them arrive at a solution instead of supplying the solution for them.

LEARNING OBJECTIVE

By the end of the lesson, students will be able to identify how they can use the trial and error strategy in fostering resilience and articulate why being resilient is important to practicing growth mindset and character development.

RESOURCES AND MATERIALS

The resources and materials necessary to conduct this lesson are:

> Thomas Edison quote

> Resilience definition

> Computer and projector

> Devices for students (foldfly.com)

> Strategy Spotlight: Trial & Error

> Copies of the Paper Airplane Trials recording sheet

> Paper for airplane making

> Tape

> Pennies (4 for each group)

METHOD

| DO | Share the Thomas Edison quote "I have not failed. I've just found 10,000 ways that won't work."

| SAY | The ability to bounce back after you've failed is called *resilience*. Thomas Edison invented many important things, including electric light. But in getting to the inventions that worked, Edison failed many times. These failures never stopped him. He kept working through the things that didn't work until he got to the thing that did. His resilience changed the world.

You might think being resilient is a gift that is unique to people like Thomas Edison, but resilience is actually a skill that you can learn and grow.

What kind of skills and traits do you think a resilient person might need to possess? *(Possible answers: not giving up, positive attitude, problem-solving skills, etc.)*

Let's watch a video clip that shows us resilience in action.

| WATCH | "Power of Not Giving Up" by KamtaMedia on YouTube

| SAY | *(after watching the clip)* Today, we're going to talk about a strategy you can use every single day called "trial and error." *(Post the Trial and Error strategy spotlight for easy reference.)* Trial and Error is just what it sounds like: You try something. You make an error. You try again. You make an error. You try again. You make an error. And on and on, until you get it. You know who is really good at trial and error? BABIES! Let's watch a baby use this strategy to learn to walk.

| WATCH | "Time-Lapse of Baby Learning to Walk" by Nick Turner on YouTube

| SAY | (after watching the clip) Babies don't worry at all about the errors they make. They try again and again until they've gotten it. But as we get older, making errors can make us want to give up on things we are trying to learn. Someone might call us stupid, other people might be better than us, failing makes us feel bad. All of that can stop people from trying. But when we use trial and error, the whole point is to fail and to learn from that failure. You can't feel bad about failing, because that's the whole point!

OPTIONAL BREAK FOR DAY 2

| DO | Today, we are going to use the trial-and-error strategy to make paper airplanes! I'm going to give you all a stack of paper, because I want you to try many different designs. You're going to record the design you tried and how far the paper airplane traveled. I'll also be giving each team tape and four pennies. The pennies are your plane's cargo. Tape them on the plane (feel free to try out different locations on the plane) to see how far your plane flies with its cargo on board. At the end of the hour, you'll choose your very best effort—the plane that went the farthest with the cargo on board.

You'll use your devices and navigate to foldnfly.com. This is an online database of all different kinds of paper airplanes. You can use one from there or create something on your own. Record each flight trial on your Paper Airplane Trials recording sheet.

| DO | Have the winning team present their plane and how they arrived at the design. At the end of the time limit, have each team face off against one another. The team whose airplane goes the farthest wins.

CHECK FOR UNDERSTANDING

Observe students being resilient and provide feedback on how they are demonstrating being resilient. *"I like how you applied the trial and error strategy and kept looking for new ways to solve the problem."* Involve students in recognizing when others are practicing resilience and how it makes them feel when they see others bouncing back from mistakes. Help build the language of resilience when students are faced with a struggle, monitor student responses and coach them when necessary. Notice how the teams that do not win the flight contest respond to the activity. You may find this to be an authentic opportunity for students to practice being resilient.

SUPPLEMENTAL/EXTENSION IDEAS

For young students: Make foil boats that float. Use pennies to see which boat holds the most weight. Record how many pennies the boats hold for each trial.

| WATCH | "Soar" by Alyce Tzue from TheCGBros on YouTube

| WATCH | "Sesame Street: Bruno Mars: Don't Give Up" by Sesame Street on YouTube

| TEACHER READ | *Option B* by Sheryl Sandberg and Adam Grant

| READ | *Hatchet* by Gary Paulsen

| READ | *Thank You, Mr. Falker* by Patricia Polacco

| READ | *She Persisted* by Chelsea Clinton

| READ | *The Boy Who Harnessed the Wind* by William Kamkwamba and Bryan Mealer

> "I have not failed. I've just found 10,000 ways that won't work."
> —Thomas Edison

RESILIENCE

The ability to recover from
setbacks and failures.

STRATEGY SPOTLIGHT

Trial & Error

Experiment with several different

strategies or designs until you

find the one that works best.

PAPER AIRPLANE TRIALS

Directions: Record the following information for each of your flight trials.

Type of Paper Airplane	Flight 1	Flight 2	Flight 3
	Distance: Cargo location: What I noticed: Adjustment needed:	Distance: Cargo location: What I noticed: Adjustment needed:	Distance: Cargo location: What I noticed: Adjustment needed:
	Distance: Cargo location: What I noticed: Adjustment needed:	Distance: Cargo location: What I noticed: Adjustment needed:	Distance: Cargo location: What I noticed: Adjustment needed:

Farthest Flight: _____

LESSON 2
WOOP: A Goal-Setting Strategy

Duration: 20–30 minutes

TEACHER TALK

The WOOP method (woopmylife.org) is a goal-setting method that focuses on strategies that can be used with even the youngest students. WOOP stands for Wish, Outcome, Obstacle, Plan. The idea is that focusing on the thing that we want isn't enough; rather, we must have some concrete idea about what we want, the obstacles we may encounter along the way, and our plans for overcoming those obstacles.

In this lesson, students will write a WOOP academic goal. Over the coming weeks, check back in with the goal to measure progress toward it. Have students reflect on whether or not the obstacles they anticipated actually manifested or if different obstacles presented themselves that weren't planned for. WOOP goal-setting is a great way to foster growth mindsets in your classroom, because the students must identify what they want and then focus on the specific skills, strategies, and learning that will help get them there, in addition to how they plan to overcome obstacles.

LEARNING OBJECTIVE

By the end of the lesson, students will be able to use the WOOP strategy effectively as a practice in goal setting.

RESOURCES AND MATERIALS

The resources and materials necessary to conduct this lesson are:

> Copies of My WOOP Plan

> Music

> White paper

> Pencils or pens

METHOD

| SAY | You might have heard someone tell you to dream big or think positively. And even though big dreams and positive thoughts are good things, being realistic about your path to achievement is an essential part of conquering a goal. Today, we're going to use a simple goal-setting method called WOOP. WOOP is an acronym that stands for Wish, Outcome, Obstacle, Plan.

Now, we're going to work together to create a WOOP plan. (*Hand out WOOP planning sheet.*) Each of you has a My WOOP Plan sheet in front of you. I'm going to play some soft music for five minutes. During those five minutes, I want you to visualize a wish that you desire. It could be about school, your personal life, or an extracurricular activity—anything you choose. You will be sharing these WOOP plans with me, but, otherwise, they will be kept private unless you choose to share them.

Take a moment to write down your wish. Now that you've written down your wish, I want you to close your eyes and visualize the very best outcome. In other words, if your wish came true, exactly as you hoped it would, what would that look like? Feel like? Sound like? Take a few minutes to write down that perfect outcome.

Next, we're going to start thinking of things that might get in your way of achieving this wish and enjoying the outcome. For example, if my wish was to become a starter on the basketball team, an obstacle might be that I am afraid I am not good enough at basketball to be a starter. You can think of one main obstacle or several obstacles that you feel could get in your way. But these obstacles can't be about other people; they have to be about you. Your fear, your worry, your habits.

Finally, we're going to make our plan. An If/Then plan is a process where you think of what an obstacle might be and then come up with a way to deal with that obstacle. Back to my example of wanting to start on the basketball team. My obstacle is that I am scared I'm not good enough. So, I would write IF I feel scared that I will never be good enough to be a starter, THEN I will go to the basketball coach and ask for advice on how to get better at basketball. Now, you try making an If/Then plan for each of the obstacles you listed that might get in the way of achieving this wish.

CHECK FOR UNDERSTANDING

Have students turn in their WOOP plans and If/Then plans and check for understanding. In the following weeks, schedule conference time to go over the plans with each student. Follow up with students about how their plans are going and revisit the process to create new WOOP plans.

SUPPLEMENTAL/EXTENSION IDEAS

LISTEN   "WOOP, There It Is," *Hidden Brain* podcast

TEACHER READ   *Rethinking Positive Thinking: Inside the New Science of Motivation* by Gabriele Oettingen

MY WOOP PLAN

My Wish: What do I want to accomplish?

The Outcome: What is my desired result if I accomplish my wish?

The Obstacle: What is the main obstacle standing in the way of my wish?

My Plan: What is my If/Then plan for facing the obstacle?

LESSON 3
Equity and Equality: Asking for What You Need

Duration: 30–60 minutes

TEACHER TALK

Asking for help can be a significant obstacle for students. If you create a culture in which asking for help or requesting the resources necessary to complete a task is normalized, students can feel empowered to achieve more. Students with an Individual Education Plan and 504 plans often have the advantage of having accommodations spelled out in writing, but all students need different things in order to be successful.

A common refrain you might hear in the classroom, particularly when you are practicing equity, is "That's not fair!" It's important to understand that the role of the teacher is to give each person what they need to be successful, which means they won't all receive the same exact treatment. But this personalized treatment means understanding their needs to a degree that you are able to provide them with exactly what they need to be successful.

LEARNING OBJECTIVE

By the end of the lesson, students will be able to define equity and equality and understand the difference between them by providing examples of each.

RESOURCES AND MATERIALS

The resources and materials necessary to conduct this lesson are:

> Equality definition

> Equity definition

> Exit tickets

> Notecards with ailments

> Band-Aids

> Examples of Equity and Equality T-Chart

METHOD

SAY Today we are going to talk about equity and equality. First, we'll focus on equality. Equality means that everyone gets the same thing—things are equal. For example, on Valentine's Day, I might give each of you a Tootsie Roll candy. That is equal, because I have given you all the exact same thing.

But sometimes, you don't need the same thing. That's why understanding equity and equality is so important.

| DO | Give each student a notecard with an ailment (earache, scrape, sore throat, tummy ache, broken finger, headache, stuffy nose, scratch, sprained ankle, hangnail, cut, dry skin, bug bite, leg cramp, blurry vision, etc.). Next, provide all students with a Band-Aid. Ask students to consider if the Band-Aid they receive will help the ailment on their card. Have students sort themselves into two groups: one group for which the Band-Aid will help the ailment and another group for which a Band-Aid will not help. Ask students if this is an example of equality or equity.

Prepare a T-Chart (or use the one we have provided) with two columns for equity and equality. Ask students to provide examples of each. (Some examples might include: Mom purchased new shoes for my brother because his had a hole in them; the entire class attends a field trip; the teacher spends extra time with a reader who is struggling, etc.)

CHECK FOR UNDERSTANDING

Listen to student examples of equity and equality to determine whether or not they understand the difference between the two. Provide more examples or do exit tickets with examples of equity and equality to check further for understanding.

SUPPLEMENTAL/EXTENSION ACTIVITIES

| READ | *Fair Is Fair* by Sonny Varela

| WATCH | "Equity vs. Equality" by Robert Wood Johnson Foundation on YouTube

EQUALITY
The quality of being equal.

EQUITY
The quality of being fair.

EQUALITY	EQUITY

LESSON 4
Deliberate Practice/Deep Practice
Duration: 20–30 minutes

TEACHER TALK

People who have risen to the highest levels in their careers or pursuits have likely spent thousands of hours studying and practicing to achieve their success. Deliberate practice is practice on tasks that are just beyond your current comfort zone.

K. Anders Ericsson is a scholar who is a researcher expert—an expert on experts, if you will. He has studied people who have performed at the highest levels across a variety of fields. Ericsson argues that for a long time, people believed that talent was limited by some inherent factor or quality—only people born with special gifts would be able to truly be great at something. This "fixed potential" view, Ericsson says, is unnecessarily limiting. Research has uncovered the adaptability of our brains, debunking the existence of "predefined ability." In his book, *Peak: Secrets from the New Science of Expertise*, Ericsson writes, "In this new world it no longer makes sense to think of people born with fixed reserves of potential: Instead, potential is an expandable vessel, shaped by the various things we do throughout our lives. Learning isn't a way of reaching one's potential but rather a way of developing it. We can create our own potential."

The role of the teacher in fostering deliberate practice in the classroom is to move beyond typical skill-and-drill and push students into a realm of practice that is slightly outside their comfort zone.

LEARNING OBJECTIVE

By the end of the lesson, students will be able to define deliberate practice and the way in which others have demonstrated how to hone in on pushing themselves outside of their comfort zone. They will also have a keen understanding of where they intend to go and a plan that chunks their practice and provides feedback on the work being done.

RESOURCES AND MATERIALS

The resources and materials necessary to conduct this lesson are:

> Deliberate Practice definition

> Copies of Deliberate Practice: Planning Sheet

METHOD

SAY Today, we're going to talk about deliberate practice. I am going to start with a story about a baseball player named George "Shotgun" Shuba, nicknamed for his blistering line drives. Roger Kahn writes about Shuba in *The Boys of Summer*, which documents the 1950s Dodgers team. In an interview with Shuba, Kahn asked about his "natural swing." Instead of agreeing that he had a natural swing, Shuba pulled out a notebook where he'd kept track of his practice. Every night, Shuba showed him, he swung an extra-heavy bat 600 times. That's 4,200 swings a week and 47,200 swings during the winter off-season. Shuba's swing wasn't natural by any stretch; his swing was the product of deliberate practice.

People might tell you that you should "find your gift." But the fact is, you won't be naturally great at anything. You might enjoy things, you might have a natural inclination in some areas, but you can't really be great at anything unless you practice. So instead of finding your gift, the smarter thing would be to find your passion or interest and then dive in with deliberate practice.

> `ASK` What is deliberate practice? (Post definition for reference.)

> `WATCH` "John Legend: Success Through Effort" by Khan Academy on YouTube

> `ASK` How did John use intentional practice to get better at singing? *(Possible answers: He got a coach, he tried new techniques, he understood he couldn't get better on his own.)*

> `DO` Now, distribute Deliberate Practice: Planning Sheet. On this sheet, students will identify a goal or dream they would like to pursue, and then identify specifically how they could employ the concept of deliberate practice to get better.

CHECK FOR UNDERSTANDING

Review the differences between practice and deliberate practice. Listen for specific cues that identify deliberate practice such as identifying an area of weakness, pushing outside of a comfort zone, chunking a goal, gaining feedback from coaches, tracking progress, making adjustments, and accountability. Check Deliberate Practice: Planning Sheets for understanding.

SUPPLEMENTAL/EXTENSION IDEAS

> `TEACHER READ` *Peak: Secrets from the New Science of Expertise* by K. Anders Ericsson

> `TEACHER READ` *Unlocking Student Talent: The New Science of Developing Expertise* by Robin J. Fogarty, Gene M. Kerns, and Brian M. Pete

> `TEACHER READ` *The Talent Code* by Daniel Coyle

> `WATCH` "How to Get Better at Things You Care About" TED Talk by Eduardo Briceño

> `DO` Have students research a successful person in the area in which they would like to be successful. Have them present how that person employed deliberate practice to get better.

DELIBERATE PRACTICE

Deliberate practice is an intentional style of practice focusing on skills outside of your comfort zone, usually with the help of a teacher or coach.

DELIBERATE PRACTICE: PLANNING SHEET

I would like to be great at:

A person who could help me is:

My schedule for practicing is:

Some people who have succeeded in this area are:

I could get out of my comfort zone by:

THE GROWTH MINDSET CLASSROOM-READY RESOURCE BOOK

LESSON 5
The Power of YET

Duration: 20–30 minutes

TEACHER TALK

"Yet" is one of the most powerful words in your teacher toolbox. That three-letter word packs a lot of punch because it promises that achievement is just around the corner. When a student says "I can't do this," correct them by saying "You can't do this, YET." The Power of Yet is the promise that the learning is coming if we continue to push ourselves, put in our best effort, reflect, adjust, strategize, and operate from a growth perspective.

LEARNING OBJECTIVE

By the end of the lesson, students will be able to identify a challenge they are having in school and come up with a plan to meet their learning goal.

RESOURCES AND MATERIALS

The resources and materials necessary to conduct this lesson are:

> Computer and projector

> Copies of My Power of Yet Think Sheet

> Copies of Power of Yet Exit Tickets

> Power of Yet definition

METHOD

| SAY | Today, we are going to talk about the Power of Yet! First, I want you to watch a video of the Power of Yet in action.

| WATCH | "The Power of Yet: Video Clip from The Blind Side" by Annie Brock on YouTube

| SAY | After watching the clip, what do you think I mean by the phrase "The Power of Yet?" (*Possible answers: You can learn if you try, you have to keep pushing yourself, etc.*)

When you don't understand something, it isn't because you can't learn it, it's because you haven't learned it, yet. Sometimes when we have a hard time figuring out the learning in class it can be frustrating, but all you have to do is call on the Power of Yet. The Power of Yet promises us that if we work hard and keep at it, the learning is coming—it's just not here quite yet.

Today, we're going to think of some things that we cannot do yet and think of ways we can move from yet to done. (*Distribute My Power of Yet Think Sheets.*)

To finish our learning for today, I'm going to play a song called "The Power of Yet."

| WATCH | "Sesame Street: Janelle Monae—Power of Yet" by Sesame Street on YouTube. For older students, watch the music video "The Power of Yet: Official Music Video by C. J. Luckey" on YouTube

At the end of class, distribute Power of Yet Exit Tickets.

| ASK | What does the Power of Yet mean to you? Describe the concept of the Power of Yet in your own words.

CHECK FOR UNDERSTANDING

Evaluate students' My Power of Yet Think Sheets for understanding of the concept of The Power of Yet. Check Power of Yet Exit Tickets for understanding; revisit concepts with students, if necessary.

SUPPLEMENTAL/EXTENSION ACTIVITIES

| WATCH | "The Power of Yet" TEDx Talk by Carol Dweck on YouTube

| WATCH | "The Power of 'Yet' with Zoe and Elmo from Sesame Street" by Khan Academy on YouTube

| READ | *After the Fall* by Dan Santat

| READ | *Drum Dream Girl* by Margarita Engle

| READ | *Bike On, Bear!* by Cynthea Liu

POWER OF YET

The promise that the learning is coming if we continue to push ourselves, put in our best effort, reflect, adjust, strategize, and operate from a growth perspective.

MY POWER OF YET THINK SHEET

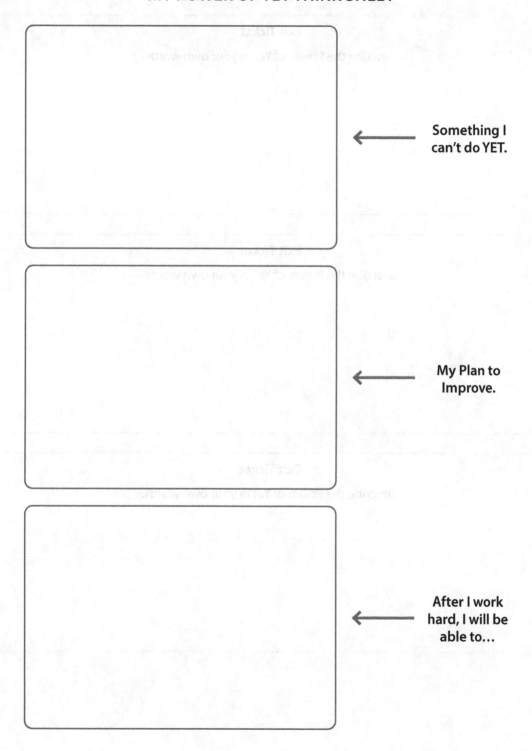

Something I can't do YET.

My Plan to Improve.

After I work hard, I will be able to...

POWER OF YET EXIT TICKETS

Exit Ticket

Describe the Power of Yet in your own words.

Exit Ticket

Describe the Power of Yet in your own words.

Exit Ticket

Describe the Power of Yet in your own words.

Perspective-Taking

Duration: 60 minutes

TEACHER TALK

Perspective-taking is a valuable skill that even the youngest learners can learn. Rooted in empathy, perspective-taking is the ability to see the world through the eyes of another person.

I want to tell you a story: I was driving along a winding road one day, when a car passed my vehicle on a dangerous curve with limited visibility. Any number of terrible things might have happened, but luckily no one was hurt. My fear quickly turned to anger. This person could have caused a major accident! At a stoplight just up the road, I caught up to the erratic car, where it was now driving onto the shoulder trying to bypass the cars at the stoplight. "This person is crazy or drunk or both!" I thought. I decided to follow the car, get the license number, and report the negligent driver to the police. Someone needed to stop this dangerous driver! I didn't have to follow for long. Because less than a mile up the road, the car took another quick turn—this time into the driveway of the local ER. All my frustration and anger melted away, and I hoped that whatever urgent medical emergency this person was dealing with would have a happy ending. *If it were me*, I thought to myself, *I would have made all the same choices*. I frequently think of this story, especially in moments when I'm ready to judge another person without the whole story.

LEARNING OBJECTIVE

The students will learn the meaning of perspective-taking and use interviewing to learn about the school from the eyes of another person.

RESOURCES AND MATERIALS

The resources and materials necessary to conduct this lesson are:

> Illusion Images

> Definition of Perspective-Taking

> Copies of Interview Form

> Perspective-Taking Slide Template

> Interview Subjects

METHOD

ASK   What do you see when you look at this image?

What about this one?

And this one?

There were different ways to look at each picture, and neither way was wrong. Every day you experience school from your perspective, but there are lots of ways that people experience school. For this lesson, you are going to become perspective investigators. The first question we must ask is what is a perspective? A perspective is a person's point of view or the way they see things. Perspective-taking is a skill where one person looks at a situation or environment from another person's point of view.

Hand out the Interview Forms. Assign each student a person in the school. Facilitate 10 minutes between the student and their interview subject.

Students will take a picture with their interview subject, record their answers, and create a slide with information from the interview. (See a sample below.)

MEET MS. BROCK—LIBRARIAN

Something Ms. Brock loves about school is:

What Ms. Brock wishes students knew about her job:

One way you could help Ms. Brock would be to:

About Ms. Brock's job:

One thing that is frustrating about Ms. Brock's job is:

Conduct a cooperative slideshow, where each student stands up and presents their slide, introducing classmates to another person in the school.

Ideas for Interview Subjects:

Special Education Teacher	Payroll Clerk
Principal	Kindergarten Teacher
Assistant Principal	PE Teacher
Superintendent	Music Teacher
Custodian	Art Teacher
Receptionist	Reading Specialist
Office Assistant	Math Specialist
Cafeteria Staff	Instructional Coach
School Resource Officer	Registrar
Counselor	Resource Room Attendant
Librarian	Coach
Paraprofessional	

CHECK FOR UNDERSTANDING

Review the slides for completeness and have students reflect on how the interview helped him/her take on a different perspective. Listen for responses that indicate they have a better understanding of the person's role and how they may view different situations. You can role-play or offer scenarios and an opportunity for students to respond to the different situations that may impact that person. Students could also develop their own scenarios and potential responses that demonstrate they understand the perspective of the person they interviewed.

SUPPLEMENTAL/EXTENSION IDEAS

READ   *The True Story of the 3 Little Pigs* by Jon Scieszka

READ   *Duck! Rabbit!* by Amy Krouse Rosenthal and Tom Lichtenheld

INTERVIEW FORM

Directions: Ask your interview subject the following questions to learn about their school perspective.

Interview subject name and job title:

Describe your job at school.

What do you love about working at school?

What is frustrating about your job?

What do you wish students knew about your job?

How could students make your job better?

PERSPECTIVE TAKING

The ability to understand how another person experiences a situation through their point of view.

LESSON 7
Get Curious, Not Furious

Duration: 20–30 minutes

TEACHER TALK

Get curious, not furious. This helpful approach can mitigate our frustration in response to many situations we encounter at school each day. Instead of getting angry or indignant about a bad behavior choice or a poor performance review, asking questions about what led to the situation can help bring clarity and understanding. An escalated adult cannot de-escalate a student in crisis, and the "get curious, not furious" mantra can help us keep our cool during stressful situations. Students, as well, can benefit from the "get curious, not furious" approach.

LEARNING OBJECTIVE

By the end of the lesson, students will be able to apply the skills for getting curious rather than furious.

RESOURCES AND MATERIALS

The resources and materials necessary to conduct this lesson are:

> Paper for Gallery Walk

> Sticky notes

> Copies of the Get Curious, Not Furious! Think Sheet

METHOD

| SAY | Today, we're going to talk about anger. First, let's brainstorm a list of things that can make us angry.

Now, we're going to practice a new method—get curious, not furious. Can you say that with me? (*Have students repeat the mantra: Get curious, not furious.*) Sometimes when things go wrong, we feel angry, but what if instead, we felt curious? Sometimes our anger makes us act out in ways we later regret, but if we stop to ask questions first, either of ourselves or of others, it can help us get angry less often and turn bad situations around. I'm going to read a few scenarios. We are going to make a list of ways we could get furious and a list of ways we could get curious. Are you ready?

Kayla brings her lunch to school on days the cafeteria is serving something she doesn't like. Today, the school lunch menu said spaghetti would be served, so Kayla did not bring her lunch. When she arrives at the lunch counter, Kayla finds out that the lunchroom has run out of spaghetti and she'll be getting a hamburger instead, which she does not like. How could Kayla get furious? How could Kayla get curious?

Andrew and Reese are walking together during recess. Dominic approaches them to ask them to play basketball. Andrew and Reese refuse Dominic and tell him to go away, they are having a private conversation. How could Dominic get furious? How could he get curious?

Mrs. Jones tells the students to turn their tests over and begin working. During the test, Mac asks Lana to lend him a pencil because his pencil broke. Mrs. Jones comes over to where Mac and Lana are sitting and takes their tests. Mrs. Jones says they have broken a rule about talking during the test and must finish their tests after school. How could Mac get furious? How could Mac get curious? It seems that Mrs. Jones got angry because of talking during the test. How could she get curious and not furious?

You did a great job coming up with questions and actions for getting curious. Now, we're going to apply that same thinking to some of the scenarios you mentioned earlier. I have posted 10 scenarios you mentioned around the room. You and a partner will go to each station, read the scenario, and give your fellow students advice on how to get curious, not furious. (Conduct a gallery walk, allowing 1–2 minutes to write down advice on sticky notes and post them.)

| DO | Hand out the Get Curious, Not Furious! think sheet. Have students write or draw a time they felt really angry and responded with anger. Then, have them write or draw how they could get curious, instead of furious, and how it might change the situation.

CHECK FOR UNDERSTANDING

Review students' Get Curious, Not Furious! think sheet to see how students would respond to their identified situation. Offer students effective feedback on the suggestions they provided and encourage them to continue to practice this strategy.

SUPPLEMENTAL/EXTENSION IDEAS

Keep extra copies of the Get Curious, Not Furious! handouts. When students react in anger to a problem, ask them to fill this out as a self-reflective exercise.

| WATCH | "Inspirational Video—Be a Mr. Jensen" by Clint Pulver on YouTube

GET CURIOUS, NOT FURIOUS!

Write or draw about a time when you got frustrated and responded with anger.

Write or draw how the situation would have changed if you got curious, not furious.

Glass Half Full: Learning about Optimism

Duration: 20–30 minutes

TEACHER TALK

Every person experiences a range of emotions—sometimes we feel happy and sometimes we feel sad or upset. Optimism and pessimism are different from just being happy or angry. As we do with growth mindset, we can view the world and our experience through a lens of optimism or through the lens of pessimism. In this lesson, students will explore the difference between optimism and pessimism and how we can use these different lenses to examine challenges and situations. Teaching how to think optimistically can help students see more clearly the opportunities that are often born of obstacles—this is growth mindset thinking at its best.

LEARNING OBJECTIVE

By the end of the lesson, students will be able to identify optimism and how to harness an optimistic perspective.

RESOURCES AND MATERIALS

The resources and materials necessary to conduct this lesson are:

> One glass half full of water or another liquid

> Half-Full/Half-Empty T-Chart

> Sticky notes or dot stickers

> Optimism definition

> Optimism Strategy cards or a checklist

METHOD

| DO | Display a glass half full of water or another liquid. Display the Half-Full and Half-Empty T-Chart by drawing a letter T with two headings on the board. Give each student one sticky note or dot sticker and ask them to stick it on the side that corresponds to their belief: Is the glass half-empty or half-full?

| SAY | I filled this glass to the halfway point; both answers are true! The glass is half full and the glass is half empty. But in this experiment, seeing the glass half full represents optimism. What is optimism? *(Possible answers: feeling happy, thinking good things, etc.)* Seeing the glass half empty represents pessimism. What is pessimism? *(Possible answers: being unhappy, having negative thoughts, etc.)*

Optimists tend to look on the bright side of a situation. If there is a big test coming up, an optimist might look at it as a chance to test their knowledge and show what they know. A pessimist tends to take a negative view of a situation. They might worry that a big test will expose them as not being intelligent or they feel a sense of impending doom.

Did you know that having an optimistic or pessimistic attitude can affect how you learn at school? Studies have shown that students who demonstrate an optimistic attitude tend to get better results. Studies have also shown that people with an optimistic attitude about life tend to live longer!

Today, we're going to talk about strategies for optimism that we can practice.

Strategy 1: Think about what is truly in your control and can be influenced, as well as what you cannot control.

Strategy 2: Practice gratitude. Journal what you are grateful for and what makes you happy.

Strategy 3: Surround yourself with people who are optimistic.

Strategy 4: Try taking on a different perspective—look at a grim situation from another angle.

Strategy 5: Keep your self-talk in check—use growth messaging.

Strategy 6: Be resilient.

Strategy 7: Learn from your mistakes, study them and be intentional about growing from them.

(*As you review each strategy, ask for examples for each.*)

To end today, I want to share with you a video. What do you think of when you look at a pile of trash? (*Possible answers: It's gross!, Don't touch it!, etc.*)

WATCH "Landfill Harmonic—The Recycled Orchestra" by Keep America Beautiful on YouTube

ASK Has your opinion of trash changed after watching the video? How are these musicians using optimism?

CHECK FOR UNDERSTANDING

Observe students practicing optimism and guide them to reflect on how they approach situations in which they may lean into either an optimistic or pessimistic view.

OPTIMISM

The ability to see the positive side of a difficult situation; feeling hopeful and having a positive attitude.

SUPPLEMENTAL/EXTENSION IDEAS

| TEACHER READ | *The Optimistic Child* by Martin E. P. Seligman

| READ | *The Dot* by Peter H. Reynolds

| TEACHER WATCH | "A Simple Trick to Improve Positive Thinking" TEDx Talk by Alison Ledgerwood

MY OPTIMISM STRATEGIES

STRATEGY 1

Think about what is truly in your control and can be influenced, as well as what you cannot control.

STRATEGY 2

Practice gratitude. Journal what you are grateful for and what makes you happy.

STRATEGY 3

Surround yourself with people who are optimistic.

STRATEGY 4

Try taking on a different perspective—look at a grim situation from another angle.

STRATEGY 5

Keep your self-talk in check— use growth messaging.

STRATEGY 6

Be resilient.

STRATEGY 7

Learn from your mistakes, study them, and be intentional about growing from them.

LESSON 9
Grit for Goals: A Story Lesson

Duration: 10–15 minutes

TEACHER TALK

Researcher Angela Duckworth has defined grit as perseverance and passion for long-term goals. When we talk about grit, we don't just mean trying hard on our school work. We're talking about showing up, day after day, and putting in the work because we have in our mind's eye the vision of a dream we want to achieve. Lots of character education programs are now including grit as an important skill for students to cultivate.

One of the best ways to share grit with students is to give them real examples. In the story you will share in this lesson, a girl named Joanne dreams of becoming a writer and doesn't give up despite experiencing challenges and rejection. This is having grit for a goal. (Your students will be delighted at the surprise ending of Joanne's story!) Continue to give examples of people who displayed grit—including offering up examples from your own life—to continue to draw the connection between working hard and achieving dreams.

LEARNING OBJECTIVE

By the end of the lesson, students will be able to define perseverance and share examples of how they can increase their grit.

RESOURCES AND MATERIALS

The resources and materials necessary to conduct this lesson are:

> Definition of Grit

METHOD

SAY   I'd like to tell you a story about a woman named Joanne. Joanne loved to read as a child. She had a creative imagination and dreamed of writing stories of her own one day. Luckily, when she was an adult, she had a great idea for a book. All she needed was time to get it written, but in the meanwhile she had to get a "real" job to make money. Joanne took a job far from her home country teaching English to Spanish speakers, with the hope of finishing her book when she wasn't working. But things didn't go as planned.

Joanne fell in love and got married, but her marriage didn't work out and she got a divorce. During her short marriage, she had a baby. When she returned home, she found herself as a single mother. She had no job, her book wasn't finished, and she was living off small payments from government assistance programs. She was broke and still didn't have a book! While her daughter slept, she tried to carve out time to work on her book. She refused to give up!

Joanne said she wasn't scared for her future because everything bad had already happened and she was still okay. She just kept at her writing, no matter what challenge she faced. As her book took form, she sent the first few chapters to a publisher. Their response? Not for us. Then she sent it to another. Not for them, either. She sent it to another and another and another, and all the book publishers said they would not publish the book Joanne had worked so hard to write. She felt sad, but she didn't give up. She would not take no for an answer. When she sent her book to the thirteenth publisher, they said they were interested and asked her to send the full book. Joanne sent them her finished manuscript and the editor at the publishing company loved it and said they would make it into a book. "Don't quit your day job!" They warned her, because children's book writers didn't make much money. Joanne didn't care, she was just happy that she was doing the thing that she loved—writing stories and sharing them with others.

Joanne faced a lot of challenges. She had no money, she was a single mom, and she had been rejected time and time again, but she kept writing because that was her dream and she refused to give up on it. She had grit. Grit is perseverance and passion toward a goal. When the book was published, it became quite popular. You might know Joanne by her pen name, J. K. Rowling, and her first book was titled, *Harry Potter and the Sorcerer's Stone*.

> ASK | How did Joanne show grit toward her goal of writing a book? What might have happened if Joanne had given up on her goal? Can you think of a time when you showed grit working toward a goal? Can you think of a time that you were successful and the steps you took that helped you be successful?

CHECK FOR UNDERSTANDING

Listen to and assess student responses to the questions. Ask students if they can provide other examples of someone who has demonstrated grit.

SUPPLEMENTAL/EXTENSION IDEAS

TEACHER READ | *Grit* by Angela Duckworth

VISIT | Angela Duckworth's website CharacterLab.com

READ | *Oh, the Places You'll Go!* by Dr. Seuss

READ | *My Strong Mind: A Story about Developing Mental Strength* by Niels van Hove

WATCH | "Grit: The Power of Passion and Perseverance" TED Talk by Angela Lee Duckworth

WATCH | "John Legend: Success through Effort" by Khan Academy on YouTube

"Passion and perseverance

toward a long-term goal."

—Angela Duckworth

LESSON 10
The Silent Masterpiece
Duration: 20–30 minutes

TEACHER TALK

"Our similarities bring us to a common ground; our differences allow us to be fascinated by each other." This quote from American novelist Tom Robbins was the inspiration for this activity. We've provided a copy of the quote below to display for students during the debrief and inspire discussion about differing perspectives. The lessons in this section have been all about overcoming challenges and frustrations, and often there is nothing more frustrating than other people! It's easy to become frustrated with other people. Maybe they don't agree with us or they are not doing their share or you just find them annoying for whatever reason. The ability to turn frustration into a fascination is a skill that can move you from a negative headspace to a far more productive one. When your students get frustrated with one another, help them turn it into fascination. Why is this happening? What should you do? Is there another way you could communicate? What is the other person's motivation? Behavior is a form of communication, so think about what is being communicated and why.

LEARNING OBJECTIVE

By the end of the lesson, students will be able to learn how to more productively navigate challenges and frustrations with other people and find ways to appreciate what makes us individuals.

RESOURCES AND MATERIALS

The resources and materials necessary to conduct this lesson are:

> White paper

> Various colored nontoxic markers

> Quote from Tom Robbins

METHOD

| DO | Divide the students into partners. Partners work best, but for an odd number of students a team of three will be okay. Now, explain to the teams they will be working together to create an artistic masterpiece. But there's a catch! There will be NO TALKING. In complete silence, the pairs will begin the process of drawing their lines. Make sure each team member has a different colored marker and one piece of paper.

The first team member will draw one line, as soon as the pen leaves the paper, that person's turn is over. (No turn may last over five seconds. You can say "switch" at five-second intervals, if necessary.)

The second team member will then have five seconds to draw their line.

Continue having the students pass the paper, adding lines in five seconds or less, until you reach a time limit you set. (Five minutes should result in an identifiable image.)

Now, it's time to title this work of art. Drawing one letter at a time, teammates will create a title for their masterpiece. It might look something like this:

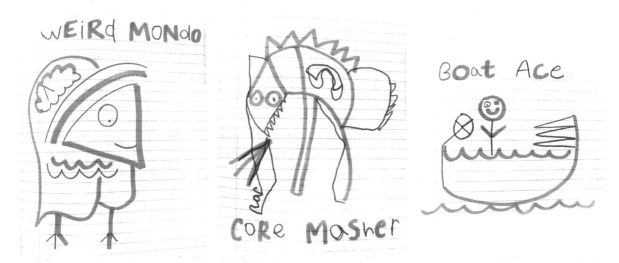

Finally, have the teams share their masterpiece!

How did it feel not being able to speak to your partner?

Did you find other ways to communicate?

Did your partner surprise you with any of their choices?

Did you feel frustrated during the exercise?

Did the drawing go the way you wanted it to go?

SAY   It's likely your intentions for the drawing were thwarted when your partner did something you weren't expecting. It's easy to get frustrated when you are working with another person—maybe you have different ideas or different ways of working. If you never work with another person, you never have to deal with that frustration, but you also miss out on all the interesting and fascinating things another person can bring to the table.

CHECK FOR UNDERSTANDING

Listen to the student responses during the debriefing session and help them continue to practice looking for the fascinating things in other people and to question what is being communicated through their actions and behaviors.

SUPPLEMENTAL/EXTENSION IDEAS

| READ | *Different Is Awesome!* by Ryan Haack

| READ | *Giraffes Can't Dance* by Giles Andreae and Guy Parker-Rees

| READ | *I'm Like You, You're Like Me* by Cindy Gainer

| READ | *Wonder* by R. J. Palacio

| READ | *El Deafo* by Cece Bell

> "Our similarities bring us to a common ground; our differences allow us to be fascinated by each other."
> —Tom Robbins

THE GROWTH MINDSET CLASSROOM-READY RESOURCE BOOK

SECTION 4
METACOGNITION AND ME

"We've taught you that the earth is round,
That red and white make pink,
And something else that matters more—
We've taught you how to think."

—Dr. Seuss from *Hooray for Diffendoofer Day!*

A simple way to explain metacognition is "thinking about your thinking." Developing an awareness of thought processes helps our students to become more capable learners. One easy strategy for teachers to employ is to constantly verbalize your thinking process each time you model a skill or concept. Students who know and can articulate how they learn best and the support they need to succeed are more successful through their academic careers. This section is all about helping students think about their thinking to discover how they learn best.

LESSON 1
What Is Metacognition?

Duration: 20–30 minutes

TEACHER TALK

Walk into any school on any given day and there is no question about *what* the students are learning—reading, math, science. Less apparent, however, is whether or not they truly understand *how* they learn. Practicing metacognition allows students to develop a deeper understanding about how they learn and navigate experiences. When students understand how to choose productive strategies, evaluate their thinking, and monitor their progress, they become more self-sufficient learners. The metacognitive strategies that students are developing today can be carried on with them to college and into adulthood. Time spent on learning how we learn best is never time wasted.

LEARNING OBJECTIVE

By the end of the lesson, students will be able to define metacognition, its importance to learning, and ways they can practice metacognition skills to help them improve their learning.

RESOURCES AND MATERIALS

The resources and materials necessary to conduct this lesson are:

> Definition of Metacognition

> Plus Minus Interesting form

METHOD

What are you learning? and How are you learning? These are important questions that help students make the necessary connections to content you teach. Model your thinking by talking out loud to your students about your views, understanding, questions, interpretations, or how to solve a problem. This helps students build their own metacognitive skills and approaches.

Powerful ways to foster metacognition include asking students what was confusing about the learning presented, asking them how their learning or understanding about a topic has changed, and providing space for them to identify questions they have about their learning.

DO Use prompts before, during, and after learning to assist students in developing their metacognitive skills. In addition, you can launch a lesson by asking an essential question that will help students to frame their learning and prep their minds to ask additional questions to help answer the essential question.

Prior to teaching a concept, inform students that you will be asking them for three key ideas from the lesson before the class period ends. Encourage students to actively listen, and list questions they may have during the lesson. At the end of the lesson, ask students to write three key takeaways gleaned from the learning. Next, have students work together in partners or triads and take turns sharing their key ideas. Conclude the activity by asking students to write a short summary to present to the class.

You can allow time for all the summaries to be read or select one or two for review. You, too, should share your three key points with the students and ask students to consider similarities or differences between their key points and yours. Provide time for the class to construct a summary. You can use these summaries to complement the implementation of retrieval practices. (See Section 3 for retrieval practice strategies.)

The Plus, Minus, and Interesting organizer below was developed by Dr. Edward de Bono, a proponent of lateral and critical thinking. Use it as a critical-thinking tool to evaluate or reflect on a process. Identify positive and negative points noted from their key takeaways. Once you plot the information in the PMI organizer you can analyze your students' learning.

Plus	Minus	Interesting

CHECK FOR UNDERSTANDING

As you set the stage for fostering metacognition, provide opportunities and specific praise to students who begin embracing and practicing awareness of their learning, who are using strategies to enhance their learning, and who are making adjustments as needed to grow their learning.

SUPPLEMENTAL/EXTENSION IDEAS

| DO | Have students practice metacognition skills by constructing a one-sentence summary or tweet about the core concepts they learned in the lesson.

| DO | Have students construct question cards to help clarify a point in their learning or to demonstrate how they can apply their learning.

| DO | Post question prompts for students to refer to as they grow and practice their metacognitive skills. Question prompts could include the following:

> Two confusing ideas are…

> I am most fascinated by knowing or learning…

> Two questions I have are…

> I still don't understand what, when, where, why, or how…

> I can use this learning by…

> The most important part of the lesson…

> I connected to this learning when…

> I agree or disagree that I can teach this to someone else based on my understanding. Explain.

> Do I need to ask for help?

> Did I get anything incorrect? I wonder why?

> How can I learn from this task?

| WATCH | "What Is Metacognition" by John Spencer on YouTube

METACOGNITION

Thinking about your thinking; awareness and understanding of one's own thoughts and cognitive processes.

LESSON 2
The Low-Floor/High-Ceiling Lesson
Duration: 20–30 minutes

TEACHER TALK

Low-floor tasks should be accessible for all learners to enter with minimal schema or skills in their personal toolbox, while a high-ceiling task equates to ongoing learning that has the potential for growth and complexity.

Can you think of a board or card game that has a low entry floor and a low ceiling? Tic-Tac-Toe, Dots and Boxes, Go Fish, Chutes and Ladders, Sorry, or Bunko may be a few that come to mind. These games do not require a lot of skill to get started and they are limited in the amount of strategy needed to outwit your challenger.

Now, can you think of a game that has a high floor and a high ceiling? Chess or Stratego may pop in your head. You need significantly more knowledge and skills in your toolkit than you would for Tic-Tac-Toe or Dots and Boxes, and you can continue to expand upon your strategic moves, thus creating a high ceiling full of possibilities.

Let's consider games that have a low floor and a high ceiling. These games have a low entry level with many possibilities for strategy, exploration, and engagement. Games such as Scrabble, Mahjong, Go, Dominoes, Catan, and Checkers welcome a lower entry level with the capacity to strategize and engage in challenge.

Consider how you can develop low-floor, high-ceiling tasks for students in your classroom as these tasks foster opportunities for students to drive their learning, engage in developing their growth mindset skills, practice metacognitive strategies, and increase critical thinking. Providing structures for discourse elevates all learners' capacity to grow and offers greater depth in thinking.

LEARNING OBJECTIVE

By the end of the lesson, students will have the opportunity to drive their learning by participating in low-floor, high-ceiling tasks that elevate their thinking.

RESOURCES AND MATERIALS

The resources and materials necessary to conduct this lesson are:

> A lesson you create

METHOD

DO Use the following checkpoints to determine if your lesson is accessible for all learners.

> Does the lesson have multiple correct answers?

> Does the lesson have a variety of strategies that can be used to solve the problem?

> Can students expand their learning by going deeper into the problem or find new ways to complete the task?

> Are students able to provide multiple rationales to justify their answers?

> If you answered yes to these questions, then you are well on your way to providing lessons that meet low-floor, high-ceiling learning.

> If you answered no to the above questions, then consider how you can alter your task to invite more complex learning.

> Add open-ended questions to your plans and offer time for students to discuss the possibilities.

> Create tasks that can generate more than one answer.

ASK

> What would a plateau think of a mountain?

> What would _____ think of _____?

Examples:

Share five ideas for grouping 16.

Identify in one minute as many words as you can think of to describe this song.

> How could you categorize the words you wrote?

Instead of providing students with learning connections, invite them to analyze the details to be presented, categorize them, notice patterns, and then determine the big idea or answer an essential question.

Create wonderment, curiosity, engagement, and allow students to drive their learning through these tasks by creating a space for them to explore. You can teach students how to apply these questions to their daily tasks and assignments as well.

CHECK FOR UNDERSTANDING

After altering a lesson by applying the strategies suggested, ask yourself the following questions:

> Do you notice students building their stamina for answering more complex questions?

> Are students more engaged in the learning tasks?

> How has the discourse helped students grow their learning and apply the strategies and skills from previous lessons?

> In what ways have you observed students becoming leaders of their learning?

> What other observations have you made?

> What are you curious about?

> How have you applied growth mindset messaging to your planning, and in what ways have you modeled that for your students?

SUPPLEMENTAL/EXTENSION IDEAS

| READ | *Limitless Mind* by Jo Boaler |

| VISIT | Youcubed.org for additional math tasks |

| DO | Create or check out 3 Act Math tasks by Dan Meyer |

How I Learn Best
Duration: 20–30 minutes

TEACHER TALK

There is a reason why journaling is often mentioned as a tool to promote reflective thinking and meta-cognition: because it works! In the moment, journaling can help us work through problems or reflect on a day. Over a period of time, it can help us recognize patterns of behavior and give us a clearer under-standing about the choices we make and the go-to strategies we use in various situations. In this activity, students will create a sketch or writing about how they learn best, but we encourage you to start jour-naling daily or several days a week as part of your learning routine. As students reflect more on their learning each day, they will come to new understandings about their fixed-mindset triggers, the learning strategies that work best for them, and how they can be a more successful student and self-advocate.

LEARNING OBJECTIVE

By the end of the lesson, students will be able to identify how they learn best.

RESOURCES AND MATERIALS

The resources and materials necessary to conduct this lesson:

> Copies of Metacognitive Survey (page 121)

> Teacher examples about how they learn best to be shared with students

> White paper

> Colored pencils or nontoxic markers

METHOD

Taking time to think about how we learn best can help to develop a methodology for optimal learning. Encourage students to think about strategies to plan for, monitor, and evaluate their learning.

Here are some examples we notice in our learning that we also share in *The Growth Mindset Playbook*:

> Annie is an auditory learner. She retains information better when she hears it out loud and often stops during silent reading to read important passages out loud so she can better understand them. She often questions herself aloud while reading to stay on top of comprehension. When her comprehension wanes, she rereads and tries a different strategy, like annotating the confusing passage to make meaning in chunks.

> Heather is a visual and kinesthetic learner and often takes notes to connect and outline her learning. She responds to retaining information by rewriting or constructing her learning in manageable chunks or in a way that allows her to do the work in some way, shape, or form.

DO | Have students think of strategies they use in planning, monitoring, reflecting, and evaluating their learning. Pass out the paper and markers, then have them write or sketch the strategies that work for them.

CHECK FOR UNDERSTANDING

The check for understanding for this lesson will be ongoing. Review each student's learning preferences; make an effort to provide resources as needed so that students may accomplish the learning strategies they outlined. Ask students to use these strategies in their daily work. When a student is struggling, ask them to remember the strategies for how they learn best and try using one or more of those strategies.

SUPPLEMENTAL/EXTENSION IDEAS

TEACHER READ | *The Growth Mindset Playbook* by Annie Brock and Heather Hundley

DO | Ask students to complete the metacognitive survey on page 62 of *The Growth Mindset Playbook*.

DO | Provide feedback frequently.

METACOGNITIVE SURVEY

Describe a time you felt frustrated learning something new.

_____

_____

What do you do when you don't understand something?

_____

_____

How do you connect new information to things you already know?

_____

_____

Describe the feeling of learning something new.

_____

_____

_____

What felt confusing about what you learned today?

_____

_____

Did you have any challenges in today's learning? How did you overcome those challenges?

_____

_____

What could you have done better to improve your learning today?

_____

_____

LESSON 4
How to Think Out Loud

Duration: 10–15 minutes

TEACHER TALK

This isn't so much a lesson as it is an introduction to a practice that you can do daily in your classroom. Students are often unable or unwilling to articulate how they feel about the learning they've done in class. Providing them with prompts or sentence starters can take the guesswork out of how to formulate their thoughts. Introduce students to these think-aloud prompts, then post them in the classroom. Ask students to refer to the prompts if they are having trouble articulating what they need help with, or ask them to choose a prompt to complete an exit ticket at the end of a lesson. As students become more and more comfortable with thinking out loud, they will develop the ability to ask for help, assess their learning, and reflect on their learning with greater ease.

LEARNING OBJECTIVE

By the end of the lesson, students will be able to articulate what they are learning and be better equipped to identify misunderstandings, pinpoint areas they need clarified, and apply metacognitive strategies for improved learning.

RESOURCES AND MATERIALS

The resources and materials necessary to conduct this lesson are:

> Think Out Loud Prompts on small cards attached to a ring or posted in the classroom.

METHOD

| DO | Utilize Think Out Loud prompts to create a rich environment for students to observe and practice metacognitive strategies. Use these prompts when teaching, and encourage students to put the prompts into practice. Place the prompts on a ring or post them in the classroom to make them accessible to you and your students and help to make sure they are at the forefront of your learning plan. Students can also respond to prompts in a Thinking Journal designed to help them work on thinking about their learning, adjusting, reflecting, and evaluating the process.

Prompts

> Today, I learned…

> A question I have is…

> I wonder if…

> Do I understand what I have learned? How do I know?

> Do I need to adjust my strategy? Why or why not?

> The additional information I need is…

> How do I feel about what I have learned?

> The most challenging part of the learning was…

> A part of the learning that is confusing is…

> What hindered my progress?

> My biggest "a-ha moment" today was…

> Is my learning different from the expectations?

> Did I encounter a misconception? If so, what was it?

> I can teach my learning to someone else by…

> Do I need more guidance or a way to monitor my learning more effectively? If so, how?

> I can summarize my learning by…

> The advice I would give myself to move forward is…

> This learning will help me in the future…

> My strengths in learning this content were…

> The moment in my learning I am most proud of is…

> Did I work as hard as I could?

> Did I ask questions to help my learning?

CHECK FOR UNDERSTANDING

Application of the Think Out Loud Prompts will determine if students are taking ownership of their metacognitive strategies.

SUPPLEMENTAL/EXTENSION IDEAS

DO | Collect old paint strip samples that show gradients of color. Label the paint strip (from lightest to darkest) with "I don't get it," "I am starting to understand," "I am on track," and "I could explain this to someone else." (Change the wording to fit your class needs.)

ASK | Which part of the strip best exemplifies how you feel about today's learning?

READ | *A Bad Case of Stripes* by David Shannon

THINK OUT LOUD PROMPTS

Keep your self-talk in check— use growth messaging.

Do I understand what I have learned? How do I know?

Today, I learned:

Do I need to adjust my strategy? Why or why not?

A question I have is:

The additional information I need is:

I wonder if:

How do I feel about what I have learned?

The most challenging part
of the learning was:

Is my learning different
from the expectations?

A part of the learning
that is confusing is:

Did I encounter a misconception?
If so, what was it?

What hindered my progress?

I can teach my learning
to someone else by:

My biggest "a-ha
moment" today was:

Do I need more guidance or
a way to monitor my learning
more effectively? If so, how?

I can summarize my learning by:

The moment in my learning
I am most proud of is:

The advice I would give
myself to move forward is:

Did I work as hard as I could?

This learning will help
me in the future by:

Did I ask questions to
help my learning?

My strengths in learning
this content were:

THE GROWTH MINDSET CLASSROOM-READY RESOURCE BOOK

Mindfulness and Resilience

Duration: 20–30 minutes

TEACHER TALK

Every day in a classroom has ups and downs. Navigating all the emotions felt in a single day can some-times be too much for a teacher to handle, so consider how difficult it is for our students. In this lesson, we're going to offer some simple mindfulness strategies. Mindfulness can simply be defined as draw-ing your attention to the present moment. These are designed to deescalate students who are feeling stressed or angry or otherwise out of sorts. Research has shown that mindfulness strategies can help increase attention and reduce stress. These practices will assist with helping students regulate emotions and refocus their attention on the learning.

LEARNING OBJECTIVE

By the end of the lesson, students will be able to identify ways to practice mindfulness strategies that will help them work toward building their stamina to persevere.

RESOURCES AND MATERIALS

The resources and materials necessary to conduct this lesson are:

> Copies of Square Breathing

> Mindfulness Strategies (posters)

> Copies of How Are You Feeling? sheet

METHOD

| DO | Create a music mix of songs that help students de-stress, a video of images or quotes, or pic-tures of physical activities they can do, such as stretching, mindful minute listening, or visualization moment check-ins.

Share the following relaxation strategies with your students.

> Breathing practices:

- Smell your rose, blow out your birthday candles. Students cup their hands in front of their face. First, "smell" your cupped hands as if they are a sweet-smelling rose; next, blow on your cupped hands as if they are a birthday cake glittering with candles. This is a breathing and de-escalation technique for smaller children.

- Square breathing. Trace a square and breathe through one side and exhale as you trace the following side.

> Be mindful without judgment:

  • Recognize the emotions and feelings you are experiencing and name them: This is…

> Practice self-compassion:

  • Ask yourself what you would tell a friend experiencing the same struggle or stress.

  • Write a letter of understanding to yourself.

> Choose a mantra or one word to repeat multiple times a day to remind you of your values, resilient efforts, or focus.

> Practice sitting quietly for one minute.

> Release the tension within your body:

  • Focus on a specific body part and intentionally release the tension by relaxing that area.

> Practice cultivating a growth mindset as you work to increase resiliency.

CHECK FOR UNDERSTANDING

As you embed the above strategies, be aware that the journey toward practicing resilience is as unique as we are as individuals. It is important to provide a safe, inclusive place supportive of students and the learning process. Check to ensure that students are responding to the stressors in their lives in a healthy way and create partnerships with families, communicating with them frequently.

SUPPLEMENTAL/EXTENSION IDEAS

| DO | Use a journal to respond to quotes and writing prompts or tasks that help with practicing mindfulness.

| DO | Incorporate time into your schedule for students to identify what works for them and allow them a chance to practice it.

| WATCH | Go Noodle Videos for Yoga (www.gonoodle.com)

| APPS | Headspace, Calm

SQUARE BREATHING

Inhale for four seconds, hold for four seconds, exhale for four seconds, hold for four seconds.

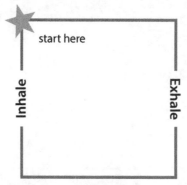

Directions: Slowly trace your finger around the square. Begin inhaling until you reach the side labeled exhale. Repeat as many times as needed

HOW ARE YOU FEELING?

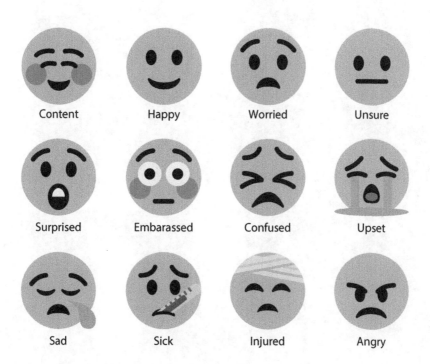

SECTION 5
CURIOSITY, CREATIVITY, AND CHARACTER

"The mind is not a vessel to be filled, but a fire to be kindled."

—Plutarch

Fostering curiosity, developing creativity, and building character are among our most important jobs as educators. In this section, we will offer lessons that address each of these areas. But call attention to these beyond the isolation of a lesson plan. Find ways every day to celebrate when students show strong character. Encourage their curiosity by allowing them to follow their interests. Stoke the fires of their creativity by giving them voice and choice whenever and wherever you can.

LESSON 1
30 Circles

Duration: 20–30 minutes

TEACHER TALK

Those in the fixed mindset often compromise their creativity, forcing themselves to edit their own thoughts and ideas because they fear judgement from others. Engage students in creativity exercises and encourage their creative thinking to help close the "creativity gap," which researchers have described as a tendency for students to be less creative inside of school than they are outside. A colleague once said to me, "When I see 30 identical drawings hanging in the hall, I think that's not art, that's a recipe." Consider your own practice—how much of your creative projects are more like recipes? Like math or reading, creativity is a skill that can be learned, but it requires effort and practice. Making time for your students to practice creativity in the classroom will be time well spent.

LEARNING OBJECTIVE

By the end of the lesson, students will have a clear example of how fixed mindsets can hinder their desire and will to be creative learners. They will gain insight into how to challenge their thinking and create creativity flow.

RESOURCES AND MATERIALS

The resources and materials necessary to conduct this lesson are:

> Copies of 30 Circles Challenge

> Pencils or pens

METHOD

| DO | This activity was adapted from the TED Talk "Tales of Creativity and Play" by Tim Brown. Watch the video first to inform your lesson. (This video is not appropriate for all students. Watch it for your own information.)

Distribute a copy of the 30 Circles Challenge to each student. Give students five minutes to turn as many circles as they can into recognizable objects. (You can give a few examples like a happy face, soccer ball, etc.)

After the five minutes expires, have students put down their writing utensils and debrief with the following questions:

> Did anyone use the examples I gave you? Why?

> Did anyone specifically not use the examples I gave you? Why?

> Did anyone have an idea, but they felt it was not very good so you did not draw it? Why?

| SAY | Lots of times people "edit" their creativity. They feel scared they won't be right or people will make fun of them, or worry they are copying someone else, so they stop themselves. But being creative includes using examples for inspiration, not censoring or editing your ideas, and putting all the ideas down, even if they seem silly at first.

| DO | Show examples of students "breaking the rules." (Even though there were no explicit rules stated.) These will include students who combined circles (to make a bike, for example) or went outside of the lines. Show these as examples of creative thinking. Have students group up or walk the room to examine the work of other students.

Ask:

> Which designs were most common?

> Who had an idea that no one else had?

| SAY | If we are using our growth mindset, we don't edit our own creativity because we are not scared to put our ideas out there—it's all about learning and growth. If we're using our fixed mindset, we feel scared to do something too silly or to go outside of the lines. Creativity is a skill that can be developed with practice, if we are able to let go of our fear of being wrong and embrace our own thinking, no matter what it is.

CHECK FOR UNDERSTANDING

Continue to create an environment in which students are encouraged to set aside their fixed mindsets and jump into the creativity zone. Have students rate themselves on a scale from one to four on how they approach tasks where creativity and expression are involved. A score of one will result in a significant amount of fixed self-talk while a score of four will indicate evidence of growth self-talk during the task.

SUPPLEMENTAL/EXTENSION IDEAS

| DO | Try the "100 Questions Challenge"—have students start a list of 100 questions about anything.

| READ | *The Dot* by Peter H. Reynolds

WATCH "Your Elusive Creative Genius" TED Talk by Elizabeth Gilbert

TEACHER READ *Creativity, Inc.: Overcoming the Unseen Forces that Stand in the Way of True Inspiration* by Ed Catmull

READ *Beautiful Oops!* by Barney Saltzberg

WATCH "Where Good Ideas Come From" TED Talk by Steven Johnson

WATCH "The Surprising Habit of Original Thinkers" TED Talk by Adam Grant

WATCH "Do Schools Kill Creativity?" TED Talk by Sir Ken Robinson

30 CIRCLES CHALLENGE

Directions: In three minutes, turn as many of the blank circles as you can into recognizable objects (e.g., happy faces, clocks, etc.).

LESSON 2
How to Grow an Idea
Duration: 30–60 minutes; ongoing

TEACHER TALK

One refrain we hear from teachers during workshops is that kids just aren't problem-solvers. Problem-solving is a skill that students may lack, but they aren't often given opportunities to practice the skill. So much of the work they do comes with very specific step-by-step instructions. Our instinct is often to step in when students are struggling by offering ideas and solutions. But what if we gave our students the chance to wrestle with problems and identify solutions without stepping in, what might happen?

In this lesson, you will be doing just that—asking students to identify problems in the classroom and come up with solutions to solve them. Remember, this is a student-driven activity. As you work through the ideation and implementation process of this exercise, remain in facilitator mode by asking questions, and resist the urge to step in and help.

LEARNING OBJECTIVE

By the end of the lesson, students will understand the process of identifying a problem and using rapid ideation and peer feedback to design a solution. Students will learn how to implement the solution and make changes to it based on observation and feedback.

RESOURCES AND MATERIALS

The resources and materials necessary to conduct this lesson are:

> Copies of My Problem-Solving Sheet

> Copies of Solution-Planning Sheet

METHOD

SAY   Today, we are going to learn how to grow an idea. The first thing we need is a problem to solve, so we're going to brainstorm different problems we have in our classroom.

DO   Let students come up with different problems in the classroom (e.g., We have trouble lining up quietly, in the afternoon the sun is in our eyes, we can never find the Expo markers, our chairs are uncomfortable, etc.) Record these ideas. Have students form groups of three. Ask each group to debate the problems listed and choose one to focus on.

Once each group has determined what problem they will solve (it's okay if more than one group has chosen the same problem) hand out the My Problem-Solving Sheet to each member to fill out independently. Give 10 minutes to complete this task. The group will come back together and each group member will present their best solution. The group will give and receive feedback regarding each member's proposed solution and then come up with one solution to share as a group. This can be a single member's solution that is unanimously agreed on or a new solution that has come out of the feedback process.

When the group solution has been decided (this should be agreed on by the teacher through group conferencing), pass out the Solution-Planning Sheet. Students will again record the problem and the solution in specific detail, writing the implementation steps for the solution and indicating what supplies they will need or any cooperation required from the teacher or classmates.

Once the solution is implemented, groups will be expected to monitor solution results. They will observe the solution in action and make notes, gather feedback from peers, and write any ideas for changes, enhancements, or adjustments to the proposed solution. Provide time for students to meet periodically over the coming days or weeks to discuss the solution's impact.

CHECK FOR UNDERSTANDING

Monitor students' ability to come up with a list of ideas and narrow it to a single workable solution by reviewing their problem-to-solution planning sheet. Check for understanding by monitoring group work and conferencing with groups to see that they have produced a feasible solution that addresses the problem identified.

SUPPLEMENTAL/EXTENSION IDEAS

| DO | Have students identify schoolwide or community problems and engage in the process again.

| READ | *What Do You Do with an Idea?* by Kobi Yamada

PROBLEM-SOLVING SHEET

Write about a problem you are currently facing.

Come up with three solutions that could solve your problem. When you are done, circle your best solution and try it!

THE GROWTH MINDSET CLASSROOM-READY RESOURCE BOOK

FROM PROBLEM TO SOLUTION

Define the problem.

Come up with four ways to solve the problem.

Choose your best solution and describe how to implement it.

SOLUTION-PLANNING SHEET

Outline your solution in detail, including the problem it will solve.

Steps for Implementation.

What we need to put this solution into action.

Adjustments to the solution.

Feedback from classmates and teacher.

THE GROWTH MINDSET CLASSROOM-READY RESOURCE BOOK

Kindness Counts

Duration: 20–30 minutes

TEACHER TALK

Children don't just learn subjects at school; they learn how to be a person. Teaching kindness is a valuable use of your instructional time. You can teach students to be kind to themselves, kind to others, kind to animals, and kind to the Earth. Kindness is an important lesson in the many forms it takes. As a teacher, one of the most powerful things you can do is to acknowledge kindness when you see it in action. Take time to recognize kids being kind, and offer a compliment.

LEARNING OBJECTIVE

Students will recognize a situation that requires kindness and develop a plan of action to help.

RESOURCES AND MATERIALS

The resources and materials necessary to conduct this lesson are:

> Gallery photos of scenarios

METHOD

DO   Prior to the lesson, set up a gallery walk with different situations. (You can do this by writing the scenarios on a sheet or typing them and printing them with images to illustrate the situation and posting them around the classroom.) Assemble the students into small groups and assign each group at their starting point. The students will make their way through the gallery until they arrive at their starting point.

> A student drops their tray in the lunchroom. What is the kind response?

> You witness a fellow student being called names. What is the kind response?

> A student is standing by themself at recess. What is the kind response?

> You notice a peer still has one lap to go around the track, but everyone else is done. What is the kind response?

> A classmate is crying because they don't understand how to do a problem. What is the kind response?

> You see a friend who did something embarrassing. What is the kind response?

CHECK FOR UNDERSTANDING

Use prompts to help guide students as needed during the lesson. Ask students to think about how they would feel if they were in those scenarios. What would they want others to do? What emotions might that person be feeling? How do they believe their kindness could impact the students' day?

Ask students to provide an example of a time someone showed them kindness and how it impacted the way they were feeling.

SUPPLEMENTAL/EXTENSION IDEAS

| READ | *Kindness Counts: A Story for Teaching Random Acts of Kindness* by Bryan Smith

| WATCH | "Kindness Boomerang" by Life Vest Inside on YouTube

| READ | *One Drop of Kindness* by Jeff Kubiak

| DO | Have students create their own photo scenarios or videos demonstrating kindness through role-playing.

| DO | Have continuous kindness circle discussions with your learning community to help identify what you and your students see going well and areas that can be improved upon.

LESSON 4
The Golden Circle

Duration: 20–30 minutes

TEACHER TALK

In this lesson, students are going to work on creating vision boards. For those of you who think vision boards are hokey or a waste of time, just hear us out! In his best-selling book *Start with Why*, author Simon Sinek outlines his golden circle framework. At the center of Sinek's golden circle (you'll learn more about this in the TED Talk referenced below) is WHY. What is your cause? What do you believe? Why is this important for you? Understanding the why can propel you forward in business, Sinek argues.

Sinek's book is targeted at business leaders, but we think finding your why can be a valuable tool in the classroom as well. In this activity, students will do a gallery walk that culminates with them examining their own personal why for learning. That why will be the foundation of the vision board. Let your students' vision board tell you important things about them as people and learners; help them understand true value in learning comes not from what we do and how we do it, but WHY it matters to each individual person.

LEARNING OBJECTIVE

By the end of the lesson, students should be able to articulate their personal "why" as it relates to learning and school.

RESOURCES AND MATERIALS

> Pens or nontoxic markers

> Finding My Why handout

> Stack of old magazines for cutting

> Internet access

> Print capability

> Glue sticks

> Poster board

> Scissors

METHOD

| DO | Before the lesson, watch the *How Great Leaders Inspire Action* TED Talk by Simon Sinek, which explains the idea of the "Golden Circle." This video may not be appropriate for all students or resonate

with all students. Watch the video first and then make the decision whether or not to share with students. This is primarily a business-oriented video, but in this lesson, we take the concept of Sinek's Golden Circle and apply it to education.

Create a gallery walk with three large sheets of paper, each with a circle labeled with one of the following: What We Learn, How We Learn, and Why We Learn.

Students will travel to each station and write the following:

What We Learn—fractions, commas, Civil War, prepositions, etc.

How We Learn—reading, studying, listening, reviewing flash cards

Why We Learn—This is more personal to each student. If they need help, you can use sentence starters like, Because I want…, Because I feel…, Because I believe…, Because I value…

Now, review the What, How, and Why statements with the whole group, and move any answers that may have been posted in the wrong category.

> SAY | Today, we are going to focus on the WHY of learning. We show up here every day and work hard to learn, but I want you to connect that learning with your personal WHY.

The center of the circle is all about purpose, value, and belief, so I am going to give you a handout with questions to help you find your WHY.

If I had unlimited money, I would spend my time doing:

_____

If I was granted one wish, it would be:

_____

One thing that makes me really happy is:

_____

I often dream about:

_____

One thing I would love to try is:

_____

One of my greatest strengths is:

_____

My definition of success is:

_____

If I could spend an afternoon doing anything, it would be:

_____

Some things I feel grateful for are:

_____

I feel my best when I'm:

_____

I think my dream job would be:

_____

A person who really inspires me is:

_____

This person inspires me because:

_____

Doing something I love makes me feel:

_____

When I'm feeling down, I can feel better if I:

_____

The things that matter most in life to me are:

_____

I would be really proud of myself if I:

_____

For me, a great life would include:

_____

One day, I see myself doing:

_____

SAY   Now that you've filled out your Finding My Why sheets on pages 145 to 146, we're going to use the information you recorded to create a vision board. Your vision board represents why you learn. This board will show your goals, how you want to feel, and the things and people to which you have a strong emotional connection. You can show this with pictures, quotes, pieces of art, drawings, or whatever symbolizes your WHY for learning and growing. You can include anything that inspires you or motivates you as a learner and a person. When we're finished, we'll post our vision boards and do a gallery walk.

CHECK FOR UNDERSTANDING

Ask students to summarize their vision boards into a few words or a short phrase, write it on a notecard, and keep it visible. (They can also use this as a bookmark, add magnets and hang it in their locker, etc.)

SUPPLEMENTAL/EXTENSION IDEAS

TEACHER READ   *Start with Why* by Simon Sinek

LESSON 5
How to Imagine
Duration: 20–30 minutes

TEACHER TALK

Albert Einstein once wrote, "Imagination is everything. It is the preview of life's coming attractions." Having a strong sense of imagination is a powerful tool in your personal toolkit. Not only does it allow you to come up with amazing new ideas, but it helps you envision situations from different angles and points of view. Imagination fuels empathy, in particular, giving you the ability to conjure a clear vision of what another person may be thinking and feeling. Imagination is also a skill! It can be developed through practice. Try swapping out an active brain break for an imagination exercise occasionally to keep developing the skill.

LEARNING OBJECTIVE

By the end of the lesson, students will be able to identify their personal definition of imagination and push their brains to tap into imagining new uses for everyday items.

RESOURCES AND MATERIALS

The resources and materials necessary to conduct this lesson are:

> Everyday objects

> Definition of Imagination

> Student Imagination Guide

METHOD

SAY | Today, we're going to talk about imagination. I would like each of you to come up with your own definition of imagination. (See Imagination definition handout.)

All of you offered definitions or examples of imagination. The technical definition of imagination is the ability to form mental images or concepts that are not present.

Simply put, imagination is the ability to see in our mind's eye what is not here. Let's try it. I want everyone to close their eyes.

Read slowly as the students try to conjure the mental image of what is happening in the passage: I want you to picture a beach ball. It's a big beach ball with red, blue, and yellow stripes. It's bouncing up and down and up and down and up and down. Do you see it? Now, zoom out of the picture and see that the ball is actually bouncing up and down on the nose of a goat. It's a goat with white fur and horns that curve backward. And there he is, bouncing a beach ball right on his nose. And what's that? He's wearing a raincoat and galoshes. The goat is wearing a yellow raincoat and black and white polka dot galoshes bouncing a beach ball on his nose. Do you see it? Now the beach ball is bouncing up and down and up and down and up and down and—crunch. Pfffffffffffft. The goat has bitten the beach ball! All the air is leaking out! The goat spits out the flatted beach ball and walks away.

Open your eyes. Were you able to see the goat? And the ball? And the rain gear? If you were, congratulations! You just used your imagination. This may seem easy, but it takes a lot of brain power to imagine something that is not there.

| WATCH | "The Neuroscience of Imagination" by Andrey Vyshedskiy on TED-Ed

| SAY | Imagination is a central part of creativity. To come up with new ideas, we have to conjure mental images of what could be instead of just seeing what is. So, today, we are going to imagine some creative uses for everyday things.

I have in this box a bunch of random items. Your job is to pull something from the box and imagine a new use for the item. It cannot be what it is typically used for! So, if I pulled a pool noodle out of the box, I couldn't say, this is for swimming. I would say, this is a prosthetic elephant trunk for elephants who have lost their trunks in accidents. See? You'll have three minutes to imagine a new use for your item. We'll share what we've come up with and then switch items. You cannot repeat how another team has used an item; you have to imagine something completely new!

CHECK FOR UNDERSTANDING

Monitor progress as the students imagine new uses for items. Provide assistance for those who have trouble understanding the challenge.

SUPPLEMENTAL/EXTENSION IDEAS

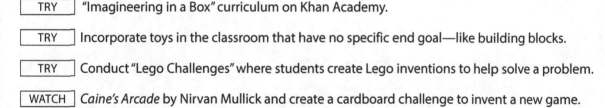

| TRY | "Imagineering in a Box" curriculum on Khan Academy.

| TRY | Incorporate toys in the classroom that have no specific end goal—like building blocks.

| TRY | Conduct "Lego Challenges" where students create Lego inventions to help solve a problem.

| WATCH | *Caine's Arcade* by Nirvan Mullick and create a cardboard challenge to invent a new game.

| DO | A "Rube Goldberg" challenge (see www.rubegoldberg.com) with students.

IMAGINATION

The ability to form mental images
or concepts that are not present.

IMAGINATION

PUTTING IT ALL TOGETHER

*"Mindset change is not about picking up a few pointers here
and there. It's about seeing things in a new way."*

—Dr. Carol Dweck

The following selection is a group of lessons that either didn't fit neatly into any one category or were overflow from other sections. All of the lessons that follow will extend or explore in more depth ideas we have already covered. As you work through the final section of this book, think about your own lessons and how you might bring in more active learning, engagement, and self-reflection. We firmly believe that the passion an educator brings to a lesson has the potential to take it from good to great!

LESSON 1
Feedback Is Your Friend

Duration: 20–30 minutes

TEACHER TALK

"Austin's Butterfly" is perhaps one of the most powerful arguments for peer feedback available. It is a video that tells a feedback story and how that feedback allowed a first grader named Austin to take his ho-hum drawing of a butterfly and turn it into a scientifically accurate rendering.

We will also introduce the RAISE framework of feedback through an art activity. Like Austin, encourage your students to go through several drafts based on the feedback given. Ask them how their work improved thanks to the help of their peers. Peer feedback activities are important because it not only gives students a clearer understanding of their own work, but also it allows them to examine the work of others. Feedback is a powerful tool for personal development.

LEARNING OBJECTIVE

By the end of the lesson, students will be able to use the RAISE method to provide peer feedback.

RESOURCES AND MATERIALS

The resources and materials necessary to conduct this lesson are:

> Computer and Projector

> Preselected song

> White paper

> Drawing supplies (crayons, nontoxic markers, etc.)

> RAISE Feedback forms

METHOD

| WATCH | "Austin's Butterfly: Models, Critique, and Descriptive Feedback" by EL Education on YouTube

| SAY | Today, we are going to learn the RAISE method for offering each other feedback, just like Austin received to make his work better. When we give each other feedback, we help make everyone more successful. What does it mean to raise something? *(Possible answers: lift it up, make it better, etc.)* That's right, we're going to learn the RAISE method today to lift up your work. To elevate it. To make it better. Although we can often do great work on our own, getting feedback from another person can help us make our work even better.

| ASK | Why does asking others for help make a difference? *(Possible answers: They might know something you don't; they might see something you missed.)*

| SAY | We are going to do an art activity together. We are going to draw a song! I know what you're thinking: how do you *draw* a song? We are all going to listen to a song together. We'll listen once and then I'll play it a few more times. As I'm playing it, you'll draw a representation of the song. Think about what the song reminds you of or if it paints a picture in your mind that you can put on the page.

| DO | Choose any song that will work for your classroom. Some ideas include: "Happy" by Pharrell Williams, "Power of Yet" by C. J. Luckey, "You've Got a Friend in Me" by Randy Newman, "Fight Song" by Rachel Platten, "Count On Me" by Bruno Mars, "Everything Is Awesome" from the *LEGO Movie* soundtrack, "Firework" by Katy Perry, "The Climb" by Miley Cyrus, "Stronger" by Kelly Clarkson, or "Champion" by Carrie Underwood.

Give students 10–15 minutes to work on their artwork. Because all the students listened to the same song, they will be able to offer feedback to each other about their representations. Have students use the RAISE method to give each other feedback on their drawings.

> Review the Work

> Ask Questions

> Identify Improvements

> Speak Kindly

> Edit the Work

After time to complete the drawing has expired, pair students and give them the RAISE Feedback guide sheet. They should work through each step of the process to provide feedback to one another, taking notes on suggestions. Then they will go back and have 5–10 minutes to make adjustments to the work.

Next, have them find another partner with whom to share the work, and repeat the process. This can be done over several days or in one extended session. Keep having students seek feedback and make adjustments to the work. When the feedback process is done, display student work with a QR code link to the song!

CHECK FOR UNDERSTANDING

During peer feedback time, walk the room and make sure students understand the RAISE process. While students are making changes to their drawings based on feedback, monitor how they are taking the suggestions into account as they improve their work.

SUPPLEMENTAL/EXTENSION IDEAS

| DO | Use the RAISE process for in-class work like essay writing, projects, etc.

RAISE FEEDBACK

RAISE up your work with great feedback!

Review the work.

Look over the work with a critical eye. Ask yourself: What is this person trying to show? Do I understand? Does this make sense?

Ask questions.

Ask questions to clarify anything you don't understand. Why did you make this choice? What does this mean? I'm wondering about….

Identify improvements.

Offer some specific things that could make the work better. Don't be vague! Be clear about what actions could be taken to elevate the work.

Speak kindly.

Speak like a friend. You get the honor of reviewing someone's work and offering feedback. They are trusting you to help them. Give feedback kindly.

Edit the work.

Allow time for the work to be improved with the suggestions you provided. When changes are made, work through the process again. You might see something new!

LESSON 2
The Habit Loop
Duration: 20–30 minutes

TEACHER TALK

In his book, *The Power of Habit: Why We Do What We do in Life and Business*, author Charles Duhigg describes the "habit loop." Our brains love routines! Once we establish a habit—good or bad—the habit loop becomes automatic and very hard to dismantle. In the habit loop, we are first met with a cue or trigger. When met with the cue, the brain goes into automatic mode, completing the routine of the habit. Once the routine is complete, there is a reward that helps your brain remember why the habit is valuable. Here's an example of a common habit loop:

Cue: Alarm clock sounds.

Routine: Hit snooze.

Reward: 8 more minutes of sleep

"Over time, this loop—cue, routine reward; cue, routine, reward—becomes more and more automatic," Duhigg writes. "The cue and reward become intertwined until a powerful sense of anticipation and craving emerges. Eventually… a habit is born."

In this lesson, we will teach students how to recognize a habit loop and have them try their hand at creating a new healthy habit.

LEARNING OBJECTIVE

By the end of the lesson, students will be able to define the habit loop process, recognize a habit loop, and create a cue-routine-reward for a new habit they would like to form.

RESOURCES AND MATERIALS

The resources and materials necessary to conduct this lesson are:

> The Habit Loop diagram

> Copies of My Habit Loop worksheet

METHOD

| SAY | Today, we are going to talk about habit loops. First, what is a habit? (*Record student answers.*)

A habit is regular practice or routine that is very difficult to change.

I'll give you an example of one of my habits. After I wake up, I drink coffee every single morning. That is a habit for me. (*Or insert another simple-to-understand habit.*) Can you give me an example of a habit for you?

Some habits are good and some habits are not so good for us. For example, every afternoon I feel like eating something sweet. So I eat a piece of candy. Is that a good habit? Why not?

Right, eating candy every day is not a good habit. But, as I said, a habit can be very difficult to break, until you start understanding the science of habit loops. Every habit follows a happy loop that looks like this:

THE HABIT LOOP

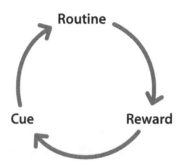

The cue is a trigger that causes your brain to initiate the habit. Waking up triggers my coffee habit because I feel tired.

The routine is the behavior that is triggered. Drinking coffee is my routine.

The reward is the positive feeling your brain has after you've completed the routine. In the case of drinking coffee, which has caffeine in it—a chemical that can make you feel more awake—the reward is having more energy. So, remember:

Step 1: Cue (Something that triggers your brain into the habit loop.)

Step 2: Routine (The thing we want to do or achieve.)

Step 3: The reward (Focus on healthy rewards!)

Today, we are going to think of two habit loops. One that we can do as a class and one that you can do on your own at home.

(*You can insert any habit loop you would like to do in your classroom, but we've provided an example.*)

One thing I've noticed is the classroom is messy at the end of the day, so I would like to create a new habit loop to tidy the room at the end of the day. How could we cue or trigger the cleaning routine at the end of the day? (*Possible answers: a bell, a song, flickering lights, etc. Choose one cue that works best for the class.*)

Next, what should the routine look like? *(Possible answers: wiping desks, picking up debris off floors, tidying workspace, etc. Make a clear list of things the routine includes with just 2–3 items. Don't overload the routine.)*

Now, what healthy reward could we put in place for completing our routine? *(Possible answers: get a sticker, play a game, high fives, etc. Choose one reward that works best for your classroom. Create a visual for your new habit loop and display it prominently in the room; make sure to do it every day!)*

Now, that we've created a habit loop for the class. I want you to think of one that you could do at home. It could be changing a habit loop by changing the routine. *(Example: When I get home I sit on the couch [cue] then I watch TV [routine] and feel relaxed [reward]. Instead of watching TV to feel relaxed, you could change the routine by reading a book or journaling.)* Or you can create a whole new habit loop. Distribute My Habit Loop worksheets and have students create habit loops to try at home.

CHECK FOR UNDERSTANDING

Review student habit loops for understanding. Check back in a week to monitor progress toward establishing a new habit loop.

SUPPLEMENTAL/EXTENSION IDEAS

TEACHER READ | *The Power of Habit* by Charles Duhigg

WATCH | "How to Change Bad Habits and Create New Ones" by Smart by Design on YouTube

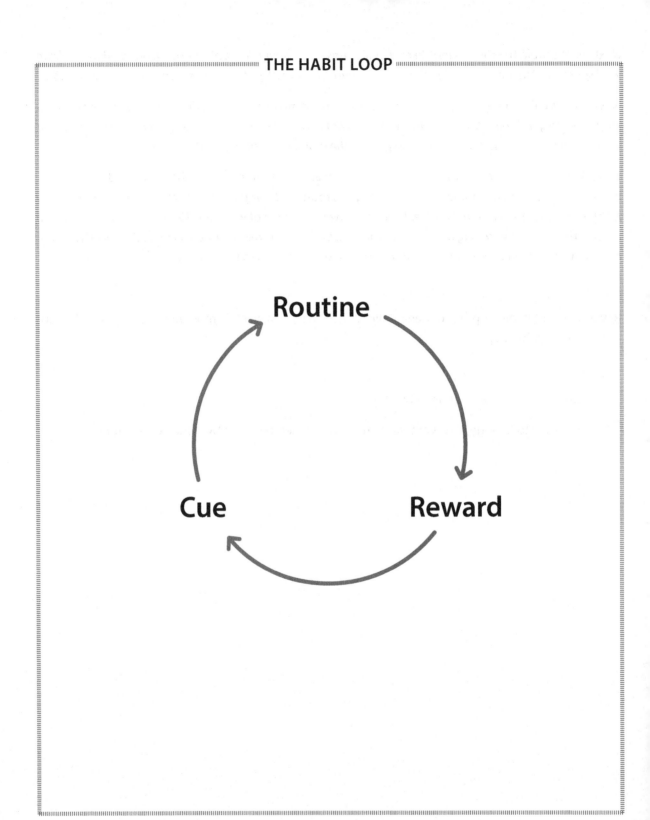

LESSON 3
What's Your Strategy?

Duration: 30–45 minutes

TEACHER TALK

"Kids just are not problem solvers." This is a refrain we hear again and again from teachers. And just as often, we see adults coming to the rescue to solves kids' problems before giving them enough time to strategize a plan. Problem solving requires practice!

In this activity, students will get an opportunity to work together to solve a problem. Resist the urge to jump in or impose your own ideas. This is a low-stakes activity where organic discussions should result in a group-created answer. The answer will be different for each team. Work hard to stay removed from the activity except to facilitate discussion and comment on problem-solving strategies. When facilitating the post-activity discussion, specifically draw attention to how ideas were created and how groups had to focus on priorities and solve arguments about what to bring. Problem solving is a life skill that many of our students are not developing; give them the chance to build problem-solving skills by facilitating this memorable activity.

LEARNING OBJECTIVE

By the end of the lesson, students will be able to describe how they used problem solving to find a solution.

RESOURCES AND MATERIALS

The resources and materials necessary to conduct this lesson are:

> Computer and projector

> "Stuck on an Escalator—Take Action" by MotivatingSuccess on YouTube

> Copies of Oh, No! The Ship Is Sinking! worksheet

> Copies of the Problem-Solving Worksheet

METHOD

| DO | Show the "Stuck on an Escalator" commercial to students. By the video's conclusion, the students will likely be laughing and shouting at the characters to just walk up the steps, but if not, ask them what the people in the video should have done.

| SAY | Today, we're going to talk about strategies. Many of you get stuck when your first strategy doesn't work and immediately ask for help instead of trying to solve the problem on your own, just like

in the video. Being able to try lots of different strategies and think about things from different angles is an important skill for learners.

We're going to play the sinking ship game. (*Distribute Oh, No! The Ship Is Sinking! worksheet.*)

Oh, no! Your ship is sinking. Good news, there is a deserted island within swimming distance. Before the ship sinks, you can grab three things that can help you on the island. This island is completely uninhabited and in the middle of the ocean, with nothing nearby. Look over this list and choose three things you will choose to bring, and write how you plan to use them to help you survive on the island.

OH, NO! THE SHIP IS SINKING

Directions: Think fast! Circle three items from the list that you will grab as you jump ship and head toward a deserted island nearby. After you have selected your three items, justify your choices below.

Flares	Sunscreen	Radio
Matches	Survival guide	First-aid kit
Rope	Bag of Doritos	Water purifier
Loaf of bread	Pillow	Sleeping bag
Hammock	Blanket	Hiking boots
Bug spray	Inflatable raft	Soap
Flashlight	Bag of rice	Fishing net
Fishing pole	Tent	Box of energy bars
Ax	Camera	Favorite book

DO After the students have chosen their three items and written how they plan to use those items, assemble them into groups of three. Have the students take turns sharing what they chose and why. The group should then narrow down their list of nine items to only three. Allow time for debate and discussion, and then ask each group to present the three items to the whole class and justify each item they chose.

I chose _____

because _____

I chose _____

because _____

I chose _____

because _____

Debriefing Questions:

Did everyone in your group agree on what to bring?

What were your priorities when choosing what to bring?

How did you feel when something you felt was important was not selected by the group?

How important was knowing exactly how the item was going to be used (your justification) in the selection process?

Each of the items you chose would help you fulfill a strategy you had for surviving on the island. Now, let's think of strategies that can help you solve real-world problems.

Now, think of a problem that you are facing and come up with three different strategies you might use to solve it. I'll give you an example. I keep losing my favorite purple pen that I use to grade papers. Some strategies I might use to solve it are: 1. Buy extra purple pens, so I am never without one. 2. Use a string to attach my purple pen to my desk. 3. Ask myself: Do I really need to grade in purple ink? Or is another color okay when I don't have my purple pen with me?

Now, it's your turn.

| DO | Distribute the Problem-Solving Worksheet to each student.

When students are finished, look over their strategies and offer feedback.

| SAY | Being a problem solver is an important part of having a growth mindset. When they have a problem that they are having difficulty solving, people with a growth mindset know there is more than one way to solve that problem, and they think creatively about finding solutions.

CHECK FOR UNDERSTANDING

Review the students' Problem-Solving Worksheets and offer feedback. Identify how they demonstrated being problem solvers.

SUPPLEMENTAL/EXTENSION IDEAS

| READ | *What Do You Do with a Problem?* by Kobi Yamada

| READ | *A Little Stuck* by Oliver Jeffers

| WATCH | "How to Teach Kids Better Problem Solving" TEDx Talk by Michael Arnold

PROBLEM-SOLVING SHEET

Write about a problem you are currently facing.

Come up with three solutions that could solve your problem. When you are done, circle your best solution and try it!

LESSON 4
Famous Mistakes

Duration: 20–30 minutes

TEACHER TALK

Normalizing mistakes is an integral part of any growth mindset–oriented classroom. In this fun research exercise, students will choose a product that was invented by mistake and present it to the class. The goal of this exercise is to help students understand that mistakes aren't all bad—some mistakes lead to great discoveries.

After the project, continue to point out when mistakes show good learning and thinking. Model how to navigate mistakes when you make one in the classroom. When students learn there is value in mistake-making they will be less worried about covering them up and more concerned with learning from them.

LEARNING OBJECTIVE

By the end of the lesson, students will understand how mistakes can be an opportunity for growth.

RESOURCES AND MATERIALS

The resources and materials necessary to conduct this lesson are:

> Great Mistakes Worksheet

> Computers or other internet-enabled devices

METHOD

| SAY | Today, we're going to talk about great mistakes. That may sound like an oxymoron to you—how can a mistake be great? But throughout history mistakes have led to new discoveries and ideas. The key is embracing your mistakes and failures and turning them into learning opportunities. I'm going to tell you about two "mistakes" that you probably are familiar with: Play-Doh and potato chips.

In 1912, Kutol Products Company began manufacturing a cleaner that was used to clean soot off of wallpaper. Back then, when houses were heated with soot-producing coal stoves, this was a useful product. But around the 1950s, most buildings and houses were being heated with gas and electric heat, which didn't produce soot. The founder of Kutol Products Company was struggling to keep the business open when his sister-in-law, who was a teacher, allowed her students to mold the soft, nontoxic cleaning compound into different shapes. They had so much fun, she suggested that he rebrand the soft compound used to clean walls into a children's toy. Thus, the invention of Play-Doh.

The invention of Play-Doh is not the only accidental invention to find great success. Post-it Notes were invented when a scientist's experiment with strong adhesives went wrong. He accidentally created an adhesive that only had a very light stick. Chocolate chip cookies were invented when a baker ran out of baker's chocolate for her chocolate cookies, so instead cut up some chocolate to throw in the matter, assuming it would melt and make the whole cookie chocolate. And the potato chip was born when a customer complained to a chef that his French fries were too thick. So, trying to antagonize the guest, the chef cut the potatoes into extremely thin slices and fried them.

I am going to ask you to research some products that were invented by accident. You will search the "mistake" online and how it went from something undesirable to something wonderful. (Students will need access to Google or another search engine. If they have trouble finding the "mistake" aspect, add the word "mistake" to the Google search to narrow results.)

Debriefing Questions:

What would happen if these inventors had tried to ignore or cover up their mistake?

What do you think you can learn from mistakes you make in class?

How can mistakes be a good thing?

Do you think some mistakes are better than others?

CHECK FOR UNDERSTANDING

Have students present their findings about great mistakes to the class via a collaborative presentation slide or individual presentations; monitor their understanding of the concept that mistakes can sometimes lead to great revelations and ideas.

SUPPLEMENTAL/EXTENSION IDEAS

| READ | *Beautiful Oops!* by Barney Saltzberg

| DO | Have students write about a time they made a mistake and something good came from it.

| WATCH | "The Unexpected Benefit of Celebrating Failure" TED Talk by Astro Teller

ACCIDENTAL INVENTIONS

Talk about a great mistake! All of the products below were invented by accident! Choose one to research and describe what the product is and how it accidentally came to be in the box below.

Penicillin	ICEEs	Dynamite
Plastic	Coca-Cola	Matches
Stainless steel	Silly Putty	Safety glass
Pacemakers	Ice cream cones	Super Glue
Teflon	Post-it Notes	Velcro
Microwaves	Saccharin	Bakelite
Slinky	Scotchgard	Vulcanized rubber
Chocolate chip cookies	Corn flakes	
Popsicles	X-ray images	

The invention I am researching is: _____

_____

The Obstacle Is the Way

Duration: 20–30 minutes

TEACHER TALK

Setbacks, obstacles, and failures are some of the most powerful learning experiences that a person can have. Do your students have the skills to turn adversities into advantages? The more we know about a problem and the more potential obstacles we can anticipate, the better equipped we will be to handle them. This lesson is all about anticipating failure. Where are the weak links? How can we turn a negative into a positive? How can we prepare to deal with setbacks? Growth mindset isn't about blind positivity that we can learn and grow; it's about understanding that failures and setbacks can help propel us forward if we learn to use them to our advantage.

LEARNING OBJECTIVE

By the end of the lesson, students will be able to create an if/then plan for navigating obstacles.

RESOURCES AND MATERIALS

The resources and materials necessary to conduct this lesson are:

> Hula-Hoop

> White paper

> Pencils or pens

METHOD

| DO | Have the students stand in a circle holding hands. Ask two children to break hands, insert the Hula-Hoop between their arms, and instruct them to clasp hands again. This is the starting point. The goal of the game is to move the Hula-Hoop around the circle and back to the starting point, never breaking hands. Time the students on how long this takes.

Once the hula hoop has returned to the starting point, have the students unlock hands and debrief with these questions.

What was hard about this activity?

What strategies did you use to move the Hula-Hoop?

Did you look at how other kids successfully moved the hoop to get ideas for your strategy?

Now, see if the students can beat their initial time. Replace the hoop and do the activity again. It is likely the students will do it even faster. After the activity, debrief with this question:

Why do you think this went faster the second time?

Did you already have a plan in mind for how you were going to pass the hoop?

How did having a plan help you?

| SAY | Often when something is difficult or we don't do very well the first time we try, we give up. This is our fixed mindset at work. But if we stick to it and use strategies like changing up our approach or learning from people who can do it well, we get better results. This is our growth mindset. The more we work at a difficult challenge, the better we become. Engaging with the obstacle or taking on the challenge is the way we get better at something.

Now, we are going to create a plan for overcoming an obstacle that is unique to you. First, we'll write down a goal, then we'll think of things that might stand in our way of achieving that goal. Finally, we'll create a plan for dealing with those obstacles when they come.

GOAL SHEET

My Goal: _____

_____

Obstacles that might get in the way:

If: _____
_____,

then: _____
_____

If: _____
_____,

then: _____
_____

If: _____
_____,

then: _____
_____

If: _____
_____,

then: _____
_____

CHECK FOR UNDERSTANDING

Check students' if/then plans to gauge understanding about anticipating obstacles and creating a plan for dealing with them.

SUPPLEMENTAL/EXTENSION IDEAS

For older students, supply magazines and newspapers and ask them to find examples of people overcoming obstacles to achieve a goal.

Try some variations on the Hula-Hoop game: Play with their eyes shut, have the group decide on a time they want to beat and then work to beat it.

| READ | *The Optimistic Child* by Martin E. P. Seligman

| TEACHER READ | *Grit* by Angela Duckworth

Reflection Connection: Borton's Model of Reflection

Duration: 20–30 minutes

TEACHER TALK

Reflection is a critical part of learning. Reflecting on our strategies and actions in the pursuit of learning a new skill can help students begin to build a repertoire of strategies that help them learn best. Reflection is made more valuable by the addition of analysis—going beyond the *what* and get to the *why*. Reflecting on what happened and analyzing the outcomes is a deeply valuable skill that students should cultivate.

Self-reflection helps students move beyond face-value perceptions of learning and begin to extract meaning. We need to help students see patterns that emerge in their learning instead of viewing each assignment, each test, each project as an isolated event. These classroom activities are part of a whole that, with the right reflection and analysis, can help students develop a full portrait of who they are as learners, and the strategies and habits that work best for them.

LEARNING OBJECTIVE

By the end of the lesson, students will be able to reflect on a situation using Borton's framework (i.e., What? Now what? So what?).

RESOURCES AND MATERIALS

None

METHOD

SAY   Did you know that by asking ourselves three questions we can learn more deeply from our experiences in the classroom and in life? The questions are simple: What? Now what? So what? With these simple questions you can reflect on a situation, understand its consequences, and develop a plan for how to handle the situation next time.

The first question—What?—is about the experience. What happened? What did I do? What was the situation?

The next question—So what?—is our analysis of the experience. When we ask this question, we're trying to figure out the meaning of what took place. Some "So What?" questions might be: How did this situation make me feel? What happened as a result of this experience? What was the purpose of this experience?

The final question—Now what?—helps you understand how you might handle the situation next time. You might ask: Now what can I take from this situation to help me? Or now what will I do next time I'm faced with a similar situation?

Asking these questions—What? So what? Now what?—Can help you reflect on any situation, whether that is a learning situation in class or a social situation with family or friends. We're going to practice using the What? So what? Now what? model for reflection in class today by role-playing some situations and asking ourselves these questions.

Role Play 1: The Test

Derek: How did you do on the test?

Kalifa: Not very well.

Derek: What happened?

Kalifa: Well, I didn't really understand how to add fractions so when those questions came up on the test, I didn't know what to do.

Derek: Oh, man. Hope you do better next time.

Role Play 2: The Fight

Jaime: Hey, can I play ball with you?

Alejandro: Sorry, dude. Both teams are full.

Jaime: You're lying! You just don't want me to play! I don't want to play with you losers anyway!

Now, ask students to pair-share a situation they could have handled better. Ask them to walk through each step—What? So what? Now what?—with their partner.

CHECK FOR UNDERSTANDING

Listen to whether or not students can articulate the What? So What? Now What? of each situation.

SUPPLEMENTALS/EXTENSION IDEAS

| DO | To extend this lesson in your classroom, establish reflective exit tickets.

> What did I learn today?

> What helped me learn?

> What did I like best?

> What questions do I have?

| WATCH | "What Is Critical Reflection? Introducing the 'What, So What, Now What' Model" by U of G Library on YouTube

| READ | *The Recess Queen* by Alexis O'Neill

LESSON 7

I Believe in Me

Duration: 20–30 minutes

TEACHER TALK

Cultivating positive self-talk is a key in cultivating growth mindsets in your classroom. Our fixed mindset is often the culprit behind that negative voice inside our heads telling us we aren't good enough, we can't do it, and we shouldn't bother trying. In this exercise, students will "trash" their negative self-talk and embrace their strengths and positive attributes in a fun and physical way. The focus is on the concept of self-efficacy, or a person's belief about their own ability to accomplish a task. Connect students' positive attributes to their self-efficacy. Let them know they all have tools to get the job done; they just might not have the same tools.

LEARNING OBJECTIVE

By the end of the lesson, students will be able to define and explain the meaning of self-efficacy.

RESOURCES AND MATERIALS

> Quote from Henry Ford

> Yellow Post-its

> Notecards

> Pencils or pens

METHOD

| DO | Post the Henry Ford quote.

| SAY | Today, we're going to learn a new word: self-efficacy. Can you say it with me? Self-efficacy. Self-efficacy is a person's belief about their own ability to accomplish a task, meet a goal, or overcome a challenge. I've posted a quote about self-efficacy here: "Whether you think you can or you think you can't, you're probably right." What do you think that means in the context of self-efficacy? *(Possible answers: If you think you can't do it, you're not going to do it. If you think you can do it, you can do it.)*

You're right. The things that we believe about ourselves have the potential to influence the outcomes of the things we do in life. If we have positive beliefs about our skills, abilities, and potential, those beliefs can help propel us forward as we work toward our goals. If we have negative thoughts about our skills, abilities, and potential, those beliefs can drag us down.

I've given you each a set of Post-it Notes and a set of notecards. Let's examine the difference between a Post-it and a notecard. Who can point out a difference between a Post-it and a notecard? *(Possible answers: Post-its are sticky, notecards are not sticky, Post-its are light, notecards are heavy, etc.)*

Today, the Post-its are going to represent our positive beliefs in ourselves. We want our positive beliefs to be sticky—to stick to us as we work on challenges. The notecards are going to represent negative beliefs about ourselves—we don't want these beliefs to stick because they are heavy and they weigh us down as we try to achieve our goals.

We're going to start by writing our positive beliefs about ourselves on the yellow Post-its. For example, I believe I am a good listener. I am going to write that on a yellow Post-it: Good listener. I'm going to give you five minutes to write as many positive beliefs about yourself—one per Post-it.

| DO | After time elapses, ask students to share some of their positive beliefs. Now, we're going to write down our negative beliefs about ourselves on notecards. Give students five minutes to write down those beliefs. After time elapses, ask some people to share their negative beliefs about themselves, if they feel comfortable.

| SAY | Now, we are going to symbolically stick to our positive beliefs and get rid of our negative beliefs. Who's ready? First, take every notecard with a negative belief about yourself and crumple it into a ball. Now, who wants to get rid of these negative beliefs?

| DO | Put a trash can at the front of the room. Line students up. On the count of three, have them launch their crumpled notecards into the trash. This is a fun and lively activity—line students up side by side so they don't hit one another with the note cards. Encourage them by saying: "Trash that negative belief! Get rid of that bad thought! You don't need that negativity weighing you down." Once all the negative beliefs are in the trash can, take out the liner and knot it up. Hang it outside your classroom door.

| SAY | We threw away our negative beliefs and I removed them from the classroom. We don't want negative beliefs holding us back in here. When you have a negative belief about yourself, write it down, throw it in this bag, and leave it outside of our classroom. If I see or hear that you are having a negative belief about yourself, I might ask you to write it down and throw it away.

Now that we've gotten rid of our negative beliefs, we're going to focus on our positive beliefs about ourselves. Point to the provided sheet or bulletin board. This is where we are going to stick our positive beliefs. We want our positive beliefs to be sticky, like a Post-it, and stick to us to help get us through each day. Everyone, take your positive beliefs about yourself and stick them to paper.

| DO | Once students are finished, debrief the activity by asking the following questions:

> Was it easier for you to write your negative or positive thoughts? Why?

> Describe how it felt to write the positive thoughts or the negative thoughts. Why do you think that was the case?

> If you were to rate yourself on a scale of 1 to 5 on how often you tell yourself positive thoughts, what would your score be? How would you rate yourself on the same scale regarding how often you tell yourself negative thoughts?

> How can you harness those positive thoughts?

CHECK FOR UNDERSTANDING

Have students practice writing a positive message or belief about themselves on a Post-it each day when they walk into the classroom. Keep the Post-it in a location where they can view it frequently throughout the day (on a planner, computer screen saver, desk, notebook, or if students are allowed to have their devices, they can create a sticky note or screen message).

SUPPLEMENTAL/EXTENSION IDEAS

For younger students, replace the quote with: "You have brains in your head and feet in your shoes, you can steer yourself in any direction you choose." —Dr. Seuss, *Oh, the Places You'll Go!*

READ | *I Am Human* by Susan Verde

Whether you think you can or think you can't, you're probably right."
—Henry Ford

LESSON 8
Finding Your Passions

Duration: 20–30 minutes; ongoing

TEACHER TALK

When we talk about "finding your passion" at school, we're not talking about deciding a career pursuit in fifth grade—or even twelfth grade! We're talking about giving students opportunities to discover ideas, experiences, and subjects that spark their interest in ways other things do not. Passions don't have to be career-oriented, either. If you ask a kindergartener what they want to be when they grow up, the only answers they can offer are those careers to which they have been exposed—doctor, veterinarian, whatever mom or dad does, etc. Instead, we want kids to recognize when they come across something—an idea, a subject, an activity—that evokes a deep connection. This is a multi-week lesson. To begin, students will identify a passion and begin filling out a passion project graphic organizer. Allow for at least one hour per week.

LEARNING OBJECTIVE

By the end of the lesson, students will be able to identify what a "passion" is and name some things they feel passionate about. At the end of the project period, students will demonstrate a passion through a presentation mode of their choice.

RESOURCES AND MATERIALS

> Passion Finder Questions

> White paper

> Pencils or pens

> Passion Project Graphic Organizer.

METHOD

| DO | Have students complete the following questions:

Something I really enjoy is:

_____

If I were to create a how-to YouTube video it would be about:

_____

If I could spend an afternoon doing anything, I would choose:

_____

Something people don't know about me is that I love:

_____

Something that gets me really excited is:

_____

I love to watch videos, movies, or shows or read books about:

_____

One thing I do that makes me happy is:

_____

One thing I could help someone with would be:

_____

<u>SAY</u>   After answering all the questions on the survey, you have created a list of things you might have a passion for. A passion is a deep enthusiasm or love for something. (*Post the definition for easy reference.*) Today, we are going to begin a passion project. I want you to look over the list and whittle it down to ONE thing or a combination of things you feel really passionate about. For example, if you feel really passionate about creating YouTube videos and doing crafts, your passion project might result in a YouTube video about crafts. I'm going to hand out a passion project organizer. Over the next few weeks, we will work on filling out the organizer and creating a presentation for our passion projects. This isn't a regular presentation—I'm not going to give you any rules; you are going to decide for yourself how to share your passion with others.

<u>DO</u>   Hand out Passion Project Graphic Organizers.

CHECK FOR UNDERSTANDING

Check for understanding by reviewing the Passion Finder Handout and reviewing the Passion Project Graphic Organizer. Monitor progress toward completion of the passion project.

SUPPLEMENTAL/EXTENSION IDEAS

READING

READ   For older students, read or share excerpts from *What Should I Do with My Life?* by Po Bronson

DO   Try a "genius hour," when students spend one hour a week working on a project informed by the passions they identified in this exercise.

WATCH   "Do Schools Kill Creativity?" TED Talk by Sir Ken Robinson

READ   *Finding Your Element* by Ken Robinson

MY PASSION PROJECT

My passion project will be about:

_____

I chose this topic/subject matter because:

_____

Three ways I could learn more about this topic are:

1. _____

2. _____

3. _____

Explain in detail the plan for your final product.

_____

_____

_____

Materials I need:

_____

_____

People who will help me:

_____

_____

My plan for staying accountable and finishing on time is:

_____

_____

LESSON 9
Proximal Goal Development

Duration: 20–30 minutes

TEACHER TALK

It's likely in the course of your teaching career you've heard the term "zone of proximal development." There are things we can do on our own, there are things we cannot do yet, even with help, and there are things we can do if we use the concept of scaffolding and get a little help. The latter is the ZPD, or zone of proximal development.

In reading, this term is used to help students choose books that are just outside of their comfort zone as readers to help them build skills and continually improve. When students are working on things just outside their comfort zone—and this will look different for each student—they will feel more connection and engagement in the learning process. This lesson is dedicated to giving students the language of proximal development.

LEARNING OBJECTIVE

By the end of the lesson, students will be able to understand the zone of proximal development and how to target goals for improvement within that zone.

RESOURCES AND MATERIALS

> Yarn

- Green yarn (shortest piece)

- Yellow yarn (medium piece)

- Red yarn (longest piece)

> White paper

> Pencils or pens

METHOD

> SAY | Today, we're going to talk about the zone of proximal development. Whew! That's a mouthful, right? Well, even if it is difficult to say, it's a fairly simple concept that we are going to illustrate with yarn. I have given you all three pieces of yarn. The green piece is the shortest, the yellow piece is the medium size, and the red is the longest. I want you to make three circles in this pattern: red for the outer ring, yellow for the middle ring, green for the inside ring.

Now, stand inside of the green ring. The green ring represents all the things you already know. It's green for GO, because you already know what you need to do in the green zone. Now, hop to the red zone. Ready? One, two, three, hop! Welcome to the red zone. This zone represents all the things you don't know how to do. It's red for STOP. For example, if you were just learning how to add numbers, the red zone would represent algebra. It's way ahead of what you can do, and you don't know how to begin. Now, jump to the yellow zone. Welcome to the zone of proximal development! When we see yellow on a stoplight, it means "yield" or slow down. The same for this zone! All the things you are able to do with help are in this zone.

As we continue our learning, I want you to think about your zone of proximal development. If something feels too easy, you are in the green zone! Think of ways—or come to me and we'll think of them together —to move you into the yellow zone. If you feel utterly confused and you don't have the tools to learn, you are in the red zone. Come to me, and together we will find a way to move to the yellow zone.

To finish up, I want you to come up with a task organizer. This is a list of things that you want to try that are in your yellow zone or your zone of proximal development. Make another list beside it of people who can help you achieve those tasks.

CHECK FOR UNDERSTANDING

Ensure that students recognize what they can and can't do, guiding those with any misconceptions.

Add this as an exit ticket response for students to evaluate their learning:

> Thumbs up for tasks they can do and teach

> Thumb to the side if they can do it with some guidance

> Thumb down if they understand where to begin or how to move forward with the task and need more instruction and assistance

SUPPLEMENTAL/EXTENSION ACTIVITIES

READ   *The Koala Who Could* by Rachel Bright

LESSON 10
I Belong

Duration: 20–30 minutes

TEACHER TALK

Research has found a positive correlation between students' sense of belonging at school and motivational, social-emotional, behavioral, and academic outcomes. Students who feel a sense of belonging at school are less likely to drop out. On Maslow's Hierarchy of Needs, love and belonging are foundational for people to build esteem and reach self-actualization. When students feel they are valued by others in the classroom, they are more likely to engage deeply in the learning because they are not grappling with feelings of insecurity about their place in the classroom or actively looking for ways those around them will ultimately let them down.

Creating a sense of security in our classrooms is an essential part of fostering a growth-oriented learning environment and preventing our students from withdrawing from the learning process because of a lack of belonging. Try to create a sense of belonging every day. This mini-lesson is a targeted approach to help your students understand one another better and open up a dialog about belonging in your classroom, school, and community.

LEARNING OBJECTIVE

By the end of the lesson, students will be able to understand how they are a part of many formal and informal groups; students will understand how formal and informal groups are formed.

RESOURCES AND MATERIALS

> White paper

> Pencils or pens

METHOD

| DO | First, have students create a master list of all the groups to which they belong (friend groups, families, school groups, sports teams, church groups, etc.).

| ASK | What does it mean to "belong"?

How do you know when you belong to something?

| SAY | Belonging means that we are accepted as part of a group. This classroom is a group, and we want everyone to feel that sense of belonging. You feel that you belong when others in the group know you and accept you as a member. Today, we are going to work on getting to know one another and accepting each other as members of this classroom.

There are *informal* groups and *formal* groups to which people belong. A formal group is like a basketball team—there is a coach, rules, and practice and game times that you are obligated to follow as part of the group. *Informal* groups are very different. There aren't any rules in informal groups; it's just a collection of people coming together because of an interest or feeling. (Have students indicate whether the groups they presented in the brainstorm are formal or informal.) Now, we're going to play a game in which we quickly assemble informal groups.

☐ DO ☐ Designate the left side of the room for one group and the right side of the room for another. Read each example from the following list and have students go to the side they most strongly identify with. (There is a lot of movement in this game; make sure a path is cleared in the room so students can easily move between sides.)

Right Side/Left Side:

cat person	or	dog person
Minecraft	or	Fortnite
soda	or	juice
Pokémon	or	SpongeBob
fruits	or	vegetables
basketball	or	baseball
Netflix	or	YouTube
recess	or	lunch
ice cream	or	candy
sneakers	or	sandals
day at the beach	or	day in the mountains
pancakes	or	bacon
Harry Potter	or	Percy Jackson
PlayStation	or	Xbox
work alone	or	work on a team
hot dogs	or	hamburgers

Have students go back to their original seats.

What did you notice about how the groups changed? *(Examples: Some were big and some were small, lots of people like dogs, most people like YouTube better than Netflix, etc.)*

| SAY | One group that you all belong to is being a student in this class. Our class is a formal group because we have rules and routines. We even have different jobs we do in the class. What's an example of a rule we have in class? *(Possible answers: listen when the teacher is talking, ask permission before leaving the room, etc.)* But you are encouraged to bring your own unique talents, skills, and characteristics to the group—we are better for it! My goal this year for each of you is to belong into this group while standing out and being uniquely you.

CHECK FOR UNDERSTANDING

| DO | Create an exit ticket for students to define formal or informal groups or to write about one of their significant contributions to the class group.

| DO | Ask students to journal about how it's possible to follow the rules and routines of a group but also contribute your own talents, skills, and abilities to stand out as a unique individual. Also, listen for understanding of group dynamics and ask follow-up questions to ensure that students understand the difference between formal and informal groups, and how individual contributions help shape an overall classroom dynamic.

SUPPLEMENTAL/EXTENSION IDEAS

| WATCH | *Purl* by Pixar (This short film has some objectionable language. Watch it before sharing with your students to determine appropriateness.)

| TEACHER READ | *Braving the Wilderness: The Quest for True Belonging and the Courage to Stand Alone* by Brené Brown

| READ | *The Day You Begin* by Jacqueline Woodson

ACKNOWLEDGMENTS

We wrote this book during the 2019–2020 school year. If we titled school years like *Friends* episodes, this would be "The One with the Pandemic." We were overwhelmed. We were scared. We missed our students. And yet, WE PERSEVERED. Within a matter of weeks, teachers across the world mobilized to continue providing a high-quality education for our students. Was it perfect? No. But if the growth mindset has taught us anything, it's that it's not about perfection, it's about progress. We watched as mindsets shifted in real time. Teachers, students, and families changed their expectations, acknowledging this new and extraordinary circumstance, and kept on going. Once we return to school, we hope to see the same growth mindset that propelled educators and students alike to reckon with a whole new reality continue in classrooms. No matter the challenge, we can overcome it with hard work, grace, compassion, and understanding for one another—and a growth mindset.

We would like to add a special thanks to Mrs. Mona Robertson and Mrs. Christi Schumaker for letting us use their classrooms to test out our lesson plans. Thank you to Bodhi and Lila Brock for modeling for photos and being guinea pigs for mom's wacky ideas. Love you so much! Also, special thanks to the students of the Royal Valley and Holton school districts. It's a privilege to be a part of your education.

ABOUT THE AUTHORS

Annie Brock, coauthor of *The Growth Mindset Coach* and *The Growth Mindset Playbook*, is a library media specialist and former English language arts teacher. She graduated with a degree in journalism and mass communications from Kansas State University and earned her teaching credentials through Washburn University. Annie previously authored *Introduction to Google Classroom*. She lives in Holton, Kansas, with her husband, Jared, and their two children.

Heather Hundley is director of curriculum and a middle school principal in Kansas. Heather has an elementary education degree from Washburn University and master's degrees in education and in school leadership from Baker University. Heather previously coauthored *The Growth Mindset Coach* and *The Growth Mindset Playbook*. She lives in Holton with her husband, Matt, and their three children.